CW00727781

If Paul Walked In To Your Church

Would He Recognize Where He Was?

BILL DAVIDSON

DENVER, COLORADO

"Our culture, our history and our personal tastes have conspired to expect Church to be something almost entirely different than it was originally and than it should be today. From decades of experience, Bill brings us back very practically, to the original design."

C. Lynn Green

Since 1969 Lynn Green has influenced thousands of young lives through Youth With A Mission (YWAM) in which he has served as a member of national and international leadership teams. He is based in the United Kingdom.

Contents

Acknowledgments

Church History is the greatest adventure story ever told. The finest chapters, however, have yet to be written, which is just as well, because some of the previous chapters have been dreadfully stained by mistakes, malpractice and even malevolence.

I am grateful to have had the privilege of experiencing the real Church. My parents, Nan and Willie Davidson, worked tirelessly for half a century to see God's kingdom come on earth and my sisters and I knew what it was to be "on duty" and ready for whatever God had for us and our family.

Somehow I had the good sense to marry my best friend. Jean is everything that a true soldier of Christ should personify. She is a leader, a teacher, a discipler – the actual Proverbs 31 woman – which also includes being the maker of a wonderful, warm and welcoming home for me and our three generations of immigrants to the New World.

I stand on the shoulders of great colleagues, leaders and teachers, from our Salvation Army days, through our years in Youth With a Mission and on into the world-wide family of leaders who now surround us in Alliance International Ministries. As a comprehensive backdrop to this book I acknowledge and recommend *"Church History in Plain Language"* by Bruce Shelley.

BILL DAVIDSON
Queensbury, New York

1

If Paul Walked In

We had no idea Revival was just days away. We didn't know that very soon our lives would be shaken in the best way possible, and that everything we knew about 'Church' would be radically transformed. We couldn't possibly have known that our friends would gather most nights of the week, in one house or another, to talk and laugh and sing and share about Jesus, having lost interest in television, hobbies, or any of the other activities we had previously used to fill our lives. Least of all did we understand that God's Holy Spirit would be poured out upon us in ways that changed every aspect of our lives, and that hundreds would find Christ. How could we have known? All we had previously experienced had been wrapped up in decent, solid and predictable Sunday-go-to-meetin' behavior.

That was in the early 1970s in middle-England,[1] fully forty years ago, but I still challenge myself and those around me with the two questions that provoked the hunger and passion that motivated us back then and made room for God to visit us so powerfully. The questions I asked were these:

"If Pentecost was yesterday, what would the Church look like today?"

[1]   The story of the Newark Revival is described in the book, 'Marked for Life' by Bill Davidson

and...

"If Paul walked in to our church, would he even recognize where he was?"

The challenge of those questions still fires my heart today as it did then. What if Paul walked in to your church, would he recognize where he was? If he was to turn the television on to your favorite Christian channel would he sit back and enjoy the show or throw his sandal (if not his chair) at the screen?

The Desiderata poem - of disputed origin - says, "If you compare yourself with others, you may become vain and bitter; for always there will be greater and lesser persons than yourself." The Apostle Paul agreed; comparisons are usually futile. He went farther by writing about those who "compare themselves with themselves," following with, "they are not wise." [2] Yet while heeding these warnings I still believe that some comparisons can be healthy. Consider the words of Isaiah, who said, "Look to the rock from which you were cut and to the quarry from which you were hewn." [3]

Not a bad idea, to compare ourselves with the rock from which we were cut – the Church which Paul knew - and ask ourselves where, how and why we differ. After all, the true fruit of Christ's Church on earth can only be that which grew out of the root which Paul saw planted and watered by the Holy Spirit. Anything else is at best some hybrid or at worst a look-alike weed!

So let's look at the Church, as it was, as it became, and as it is, in order to make comparisons from which we might draw conclusions for the present and plans for the future. Granted, this will be from my perspective. I have only been in ministry for fifty years and have merely glimpsed the Church in about thirty countries, so my horizons are limited. Readers must draw their own conclusions.

---

2   2 Corinthians 10:12,13
3   Isaiah 51:1

Perhaps comparing the modern Church with its roots is unreasonable. The world has changed almost entirely since the days when the First Church burst onto the streets of Jerusalem. At the time of writing it is the year Queen Elizabeth II celebrates the 60th anniversary of the day she ascended to the throne upon the death of her father, King George VI. At the moment of ascension, the time of the King's death, she was sitting on a look-out platform in a Kenyan Safari Park. Hearing the news, she made arrangements to fly back to London where her octogenarian Prime Minister, Sir Winston Churchill, waited to greet her at the foot of the steps of the Royal Plane. The twenty-four-year-old Queen, greeted by a man who participated in the last horse and cavalry charge of the British Army!

Think of it! Churchill belonged to the era when men made war using the same tactics and many of the weapons as did King David of Judah! Now Queen Elizabeth still reigns in an age when robotic weapons of mass destruction are flying over Arabian deserts, operated by young men and women sitting in control rooms in California who go home after work to enjoy dinner with their families. I was seven years old when Elizabeth was crowned. How the world has changed since what seems to me like 'only yesterday'!

Can we make sensible comparisons between our generation and the Church of the New Testament? Is there any value in the attempt? At least let's inspect the root to make sure we have its fruit. Let's be radical, and that doesn't mean – as we thought it did in the 1960s – to tear down the worst without any idea how to build up the better or the best. The word *radical* is less revolutionary than we have given its meaning. It comes from the Latin word for *root,* and when it comes to the Church, we'd best not tear up or somehow lose the life from that original root, lest we lose all meaning and purpose. So, for better or for worse, let's compare our fruit with our root.

Introducing Life Group Discussion

You might be reading this book alone, or as part of a small group project. Either way, these 'talk-back' pages will help you digest and apply each idea as you walk through the chapters. I encourage you to find a small group – we call them Life Groups. If you don't know of one, then what are you waiting for? Be a host to a Life Group and – among other things - enjoy a far more dynamic approach to reading 'as iron sharpens iron'.

To get things started, the leader or host of your group might like to read the opening paragraphs of each Life Group Discussion session. I've written them as if I'm that person. Once the discussion gets going, you'll probably find plenty of healthy momentum as you bounce your opinions and ideas around.

One last point; never end without praying for one another.

Have fun… be blessed, be encouraged…

Bill Davidson

Life Group Discussion
Chapter 1: If Paul Walked In

Jesus told a story about a Pharisee who stood up in the temple and prayed, "God, I thank you that I am not like other men — robbers, evildoers, adulterers — or even like this tax collector. I fast twice a week and give a tenth of all I get." [4] He obviously enjoyed making favorable comparisons! Of course, if that is your goal, you will only be content when relating to people you consider inferior to yourself!

Paul speaks of the foolishness of comparing ourselves with ourselves or with others. [5] The quotation in this chapter from *Desiderata* adds another warning: "If you compare yourself with others, you may become vain and bitter; for always there will be greater and lesser persons than yourself."

We have three situations described in the verses above.
   a.   A man comparing himself with someone of lesser stature than himself.
   b.   People who compare themselves with themselves.
   c.   Those who compare themselves with others to gauge their value or status.

Questions for Discussion
   1.   What character qualities, such as Pride, Futility, Competitiveness, Criticism, Insecurity, etc., - would you attribute to each of these situations?

To discover a healthier use of comparison, let's read Psalm 119:72; Proverbs 3:13-15, and Psalm 89:6. In these verses we see that we can use comparison to make healthy evaluations of things in our world and in our lives.

---

4   Luke 18:11,12
5   2 Corinthians 10:12-18

2. What are the differences in spirit and attitude between these contrasting uses of comparison?

3. In the following chapters Bill makes comparisons between the modern Church and the Church of the New Testament age. What do you expect to find? Do you think we will do well by comparison? Can you begin to guess what differences we might discover? Talk about it together before you read on.

2

The Way We Were

In *"Church History in Plain Language,"* Bruce Shelley opens with a smile. He refers to those great kids in the Peanuts strip who had a way of making profound, even prophetic statements from time to time. I think it comes from spending so much time with such a wise dog.

Charlie Brown's sister, Sally, is pictured writing a project for school. It's titled "Church History" and she begins, "When writing about church history we have to go back to the very beginning. Our pastor was born in 1930." The Church, however, had a somewhat earlier genesis.

If we start at the very beginning – a very good place to start – we must own up to our Jewish roots. We began as a sect of Judaism and might have remained so had it not been for certain events, provoked no doubt by nothing less than God's sovereignty, for it was never His plan for our spiritual forefathers to be closeted in the back room of a synagogue or lost among the ramblings of generations of rabbinic speculation. The Church, as with all its members, would be born of the Spirit and not by a continuation of tradition or human interpretation of the Law.

The Church's umbilical cord began to be severed by the one event which defines its identity and upon which everything it stands for depends. Paul was clear on the subject. The resurrection of Christ and the subsequent hope that every Christian would be raised up into eternal life is the foundation upon which everything else in the Church is built.

> *"But if it is preached that Christ has been raised from the dead,*
> *how can some of you say that there is no resurrection of the dead?*
> *If there is no resurrection of the dead, then not even Christ has been raised.*
> *And if Christ has not been raised, our preaching is useless and so is your faith.*
> *More than that, we are then found to be false witnesses about God,*
> *for we have testified about God that he raised Christ from the dead.*
> *But he did not raise him if in fact the dead are not raised.*
> *For if the dead are not raised, then Christ has not been raised either.*
> *And if Christ has not been raised, your faith is futile; you are still in your sins."* [6]

The first apostles never struggled, as we often do, to fit their message to the prevailing culture and philosophical climate of their times. How could they? At the very root of their message was an absurdity. They claimed that God Himself had not only appeared to human-kind but had also taken upon Himself both the offense and the punishment exacted by His own law, had died in man's place and risen from the dark place of death, showing Himself to hundreds of witnesses. [7]

To believe this was the basis of being a Christian, and it immediately set Christianity at odds with the religious status quo. To understand this we must take a few steps back from the time of Christ's crucifixion, even beyond His ministry and birth to visit the silent years between Malachi and Matthew; between the Old Testament and the New.

The last words of the Old Testament proclaimed both a promise and a warning. "See, I will send you the prophet Elijah before that great and dreadful day of the Lord comes. He will turn the hearts of the fathers

---

6   1 Corinthians 15:12-17
7   1 Corinthians 15:3-8

to their children, and the hearts of the children to their fathers; or else I will come and strike the land with a curse." [8] Four hundred years later the Angel Gabriel echoed those words when describing the child soon to be born to Elizabeth, a direct descendant of the priestly Aaronic line and the wife of a priest called Zechariah. The child in question would become known as The Baptist. His name was John. [9]

Luke describes Zachariah and Elizabeth as 'upright in the sight of God'. No doubt the same could be said of others of the priestly line, but not for all. The Old Testament ended after the restoration of Jerusalem and the priesthood, but those long and dark generations between the testaments saw the priesthood become little more than a political office. Divisions within it were not those devised by earlier generations dating back to the time of Moses and Aaron, they were now merely divisions of power-politics and even deeper divisions over doctrine. The Pharisees, Sadducees and Herodians ruled by money, power and politics. Over them stood the Pax Romana, [10] a peace only enjoyed by those who submitted to the rule of Rome.

Into this darkness God shed His light. As the apostle John put it, "the light shone in the darkness, but the darkness did not take readily to it." [11] That's putting it mildly. From the outset of His ministry Jesus was at odds with the culture of compromise and political expediency which had grown like creeping ivy on the face of the temple walls. On one visit to the temple Jesus overturned the tables of the money changers and the benches of those selling doves. "It is written," he said to them, "My house will be called a house of prayer, but you are making it a den of robbers." [12]

We are accustomed to using the words that Jesus spoke about new

---

8   Malachi 4:5,6
9   Luke 1:16,17
10   Pax Romana means 'The Roman Peace' – the relative state of peace brought about by the authoritarian rule of the Roman Emprire.
11   John 1:5
12   Matthew 21:13

wine in old wineskins for our own purposes and to suit our own ends, especially when we like to think that the 'new wine' refers to the outpouring of the Holy Spirit in our lives. That this outpouring is part of the picture is beyond question, but put in its original context the old wine referred to a condemnation of Judaism as Jesus found it.

It was the disciples of John the Baptist who started the conversation.

"How is it that we and the Pharisees fast, but your disciples do not fast?"

"How can the guests of the bridegroom mourn," Jesus answered, "while he is with them? The time will come when the bridegroom will be taken from them; then they will fast. No one sews a patch of unshrunk cloth on an old garment, for the patch will pull away from the garment, making the tear worse. Neither do men pour new wine into old wineskins. If they do, the skins will burst, the wine will run out and the wineskins will be ruined. No, they pour new wine into new wineskins, and both are preserved." [13]

For those who would casually set Judaism aside at this point it is worth a mention that Jesus said, "Both are preserved." He made no mention of preserving the new bottle, full of its new wine, while discarding the old, complete with its contents, to the recycling dump of history. Nevertheless, a clear distinction had been made. It was a cup of this old wine that Jesus picked up on the night of the Last Supper, the fourth cup of the Passover Celebration, and He transformed it into the cup of the "new covenant in my blood." "Do this," He said, "whenever you drink it, in remembrance of me." [14] Notice, he said that when we partake of this cup it will no longer be in remembrance of the *type* of salvation - the Passover and the deliverance out of the slavery of Egypt - but would now be the *reality* of deliverance through the shedding of

---

13 Matthew 9:14-17
14 1 Corinthians 11:25

His blood. He was saying; from this day on you have a new and more complete reason to partake of this cup, in spirit and in truth.

In every season of transition there are those who stand at the bow of the ship, full of excited expectation, like Rose and Jack on the prow of the Titanic. But then there are those who sit huddled on the aft deck, looking fondly back on what they've left behind. So it was with the Early Church. Being predominantly Jewish, Judaism pervaded every step they took, every thought that crossed their minds and every word that passed their lips. From the first cutting of the knife in circumcision to the last breath on earth, a man was first and foremost a Jew and the Church to which he belonged – at least in the earliest days of Christianity – was a Jewish sect. They were, for better or for worse, new wine in an old bottle. Inevitably, the cork would one day pop.

In some ways the new wine had already begun to thrive outside the old bottle. The Church's witness to the resurrection of Jesus did not belong in the old wineskin; neither could it be forced to be bottled up within it. However, if the resurrection was beyond doubt there were other issues which were anything but agreed upon within the Early Church.

It is surprising that the man who tried to stubbornly preserve the Jewish root of the Church was not Saul of Tarsus, the one who described himself as "circumcised on the eighth day, of the people of Israel, of the tribe of Benjamin, a Hebrew of Hebrews; in regard to the law, a Pharisee," [15] and "I am a Pharisee, the son of a Pharisee." [16] It was the unschooled fisherman, Peter, who hung back, strangely fixed in his Jewish ways.

Paul's opposition to Peter was strong and to the point. "When Peter came to Antioch, I opposed him to his face, because he was clearly in the wrong. Before certain men came from James, he used to eat

---

15 Philippians 3:5
16 Acts 23:6

with the Gentiles. But when they arrived, he began to draw back and separate himself from the Gentiles because he was afraid of those who belonged to the circumcision group. The other Jews joined him in his hypocrisy, so that by their hypocrisy even Barnabas was led astray." [17]

Peter showed a remarkable forgetfulness on this issue, failing to recall the things Jesus had said and done. He even forgot the great occasion when a Roman Centurion approached Jesus to ask help for his servant who lay at home, paralyzed and in pain. Immediately Jesus responded, "I will go and heal him." [18] In that statement He broke the taboo of a Jew entering the home and receiving the hospitality of a Gentile – especially a Gentile who wore the cloak and armor of Rome. However, by the time we get to the tenth chapter of the book of Acts it took a prophetic dream and a direct rebuke from God before Peter was ready to risk associating with a Centurion, even though the Roman and his entire household were described as "devout and God-fearing." [19]

Later, when Peter was rebuked by fellow Jewish members of the Church, he scrambled to defend himself.

"You went into the house of uncircumcised men and ate with them," the Jewish believers charged.

Peter pointed out that he had argued with God over the idea of such an act.

"I replied, 'Surely not, Lord! Nothing impure or unclean has ever entered my mouth.'" [20] Perhaps if he made it plain he was not easily persuaded by God, it gave him an excuse for his liberalness!

However, it was another phenomenon that finally separated the Church

---

17   Galatians 2:11-13
18   Matthew 8:7
19   Acts 10:1
20   Acts 11:3-8

from its position as a Jewish sect. During his ministry, Jesus clearly foretold of events, some of which would soon happen in Jerusalem and others at the time of His triumphant return. He added, "I tell you the truth, this generation will certainly not pass away until all these things have happened." [21] Jesus prophesied that the temple itself would be desecrated and an abominable sight would be seen before the holy altar. He continued, "So when you see standing in the holy place 'the abomination that causes desolation,' spoken of through the prophet Daniel — let the reader understand — then let those who are in Judea flee to the mountains. Let no one on the roof of his house go down to take anything out of the house. Let no one in the field go back to get his cloak. How dreadful it will be in those days for pregnant women and nursing mothers! Pray that your flight will not take place in winter or on the Sabbath." [22]

In AD 66, only thirty years after Jesus spoke those words, the citizens of Jerusalem attempted to break free from their Roman overlords. Rome responded with a fury which made earlier seasons of occupation, difficult as they had been, seem like a forgotten dream. In AD 70, almost one biblical generation after Christ's death, the Emperor Vespasian's armies broke through Jerusalem's defenses and stormed the temple, looting it of its holy stores and burning it to the ground. Within days every synagogue in the region of Palestine was utterly destroyed. Urged on by memories of Christ's words and the leaders of the Church, the Christians obediently ran from the city. Understandably, their flight was seen by the Jews who remained as a cowardly retreat – no less than an act of treason.

Before that time, however, the Church in Jerusalem had established a lifestyle which in many ways reflected its Jewish roots, with its emphasis on family, relationships, common meals and clan fidelity. Here we may begin to compare ourselves with that Early Church and ask whether we have preserved or lost such qualities.

---

21   Matthew 24:34
22   Matthew 24:15

For instance, consider the time when the Church elders in Jerusalem were confronted with a complaint from the Hellenistic [23] believers. These *Hellenists* were, by definition, Greek or non-Jewish believers. Many of them had been converts to the Jewish faith before they found Christ and joined the Church. Some might have traveled to Jerusalem for the celebration of Pentecost only to find themselves confronted by the challenge of Peter's first sermon at the birth of the Church.

As these Gentile believers were assimilated into the Church, certain cultural differences became obvious. We pick up the story in the sixth chapter of Acts. "In those days when the number of disciples was increasing, the Grecian Jews among them complained against the Hebraic Jews because their widows were being overlooked in the daily distribution of food. So the Twelve gathered all the disciples together and said, 'It would not be right for us to neglect the ministry of the word of God in order to wait on tables. Brothers, choose seven men from among you who are known to be full of the Spirit and wisdom. We will turn this responsibility over to them and will give our attention to prayer and the ministry of the word.'" [24]

At first glance, this problem might appear to be nothing short of racism in the midst of the first Christian community. But consider this; the Jewish believers were influenced not only by the negatives of Judaist legalism, but also by the many positive qualities of community which had been injected into their culture at its earliest stages by God Himself. To them, community meant family, tribe, clan. To the Greek it might have felt more like organization, politics and democracy.

Brought up in the ways of the Jewish scriptures, Hebrew believers would have been acquainted with those cross-sections where the law invaded the attitude of the heart. It was common for them to look after those in their midst who might otherwise have suffered. Were the

---

23   *Hellenistic* comes from the word, 'Greek,' *Ellada* (Ελλάδα), and the term for 'Greece,' *Hellas* (Ελλάς)
24   Acts 6:1-4

Hellenists lacking in this department? It would seem so as they complained about their widows being neglected in the welfare program of the Church. I wonder if the apostles were shocked. I can almost hear them saying, "You mean you don't automatically look after your widows, as is our custom?"

Jewish believers had been schooled in the practice of mercy toward the afflicted. The second writing of the law in the book of Deuteronomy said this: "When you have finished setting aside a tenth of all your produce in the third year, the year of the tithe, you shall give it to the Levite, the alien, the fatherless and the widow, so that they may eat in your towns and be satisfied." [25] God spoke of this through Isaiah; "Defend the cause of the fatherless, plead the case of the widow." [26] And the ancient book of Job stated, "The man who was dying blessed me; I made the widow's heart sing." [27] Paul wrote to Timothy, reflecting this old Jewish attitude of grace into the growing Gentile church: "Give proper recognition to those widows who are really in need." [28]

Add to that quality of family, clan and community, the amazing dedication and commitment of those earliest believers. Luke, the writer of the Book of Acts, described them this way: "They devoted themselves to the apostles' teaching and to the fellowship, to the breaking of bread and to prayer. Everyone was filled with awe, and many wonders and miraculous signs were done by the apostles. All the believers were together and had everything in common. Selling their possessions and goods, they gave to anyone as he had need. Every day they continued to meet together in the temple courts. They broke bread in their homes and ate together with glad and sincere hearts, praising God and enjoying the favor of all the people." [29]

The members of the first Church were an extraordinary group of

---

25   Deuteronomy 26:12
26   Isaiah 1:17
27   Job 29:13
28   1 Timothy 5:3
29   Acts 2:42-47

people. Consider this description and compare it with our contemporary Church: "No one else dared join them, even though they were highly regarded by the people. Nevertheless, more and more men and women believed in the Lord and were added to their number." [30]

Dare we compare? Is there a Christian Church in your neighborhood where it might be said, "There were no needy persons among them. For from time to time those who owned lands or houses sold them, brought the money from the sales and put it at the apostles' feet, and it was distributed to anyone as he had need?" [31]

Perhaps, nowadays, we don't need that level of commitment. If people are truly in need In the Western World there are welfare agencies somewhere in town. Who needs the Church when we've got the State! But this extraordinary New Testament community is who we were. And so we must ask the tough question, "Would we be recognized, if Paul walked in?"

See the Church standing empty, see the Church standing bare.
You can empty it of people if you empty it of care
And if Jesus was in need would He find a hand-out there?
Or would He just see Good Friday, all over again? [32]

---

30   Acts 5:13,14
31   Acts 4:33-35
32   From, Good Friday (All over again) by Bill Davidson – from the album Star Wars of Darkness & Light – Pilgrim Records 1978.

Life Group Discussion
Chapter 2: The Way We Were

Let's begin this talk-back session with some questions:

1. The first people to experience life in the Church were mainly Jewish believers. That was our root. What were the first two causes for the Church separating from its Jewish origins?

2. In the generations between the Old and New Testaments, what major changes took place in Judaism?

3. When Jesus used the metaphor of the Old and New Wine, to what was He referring? And did He suggest we throw out the old?

4. What was the Old Testament 'type' of salvation represented by the cup Jesus took up during the Last Supper, and into what did He transform its representation?

The section of this chapter which referred to the dispute over the Hellenistic widows is found in Acts 6:1-4. Let's have someone from the group read those verses and Acts 2:42-47, then discuss the following questions.

5. What sort of lifestyle do these verses suggest? How did the Church live, on a day-by-day basis?

6. What level of commitment did this lifestyle demand? Is it in any way possible for us to have a similar depth of commitment to one another in the modern Church?

Lord Jesus,
We know You love Your Church. Help us to love it in like manner.
Show us how to express that love not only in words, but in real life actions.

3

The Silent Church

One description of the Early Church impresses me more than all others. No, it's not the long list of miracles, they were God's doing. It is the report of what happened when the Church was suddenly and viciously attacked, then scattered.

Opposition to the news of Christ's life, death and resurrection as told by the apostles had been a factor since the earliest days of their preaching. Even the first Christian sermon was met with a mixed reception: "Amazed and perplexed, they asked one another, 'What does this mean?' Some, however, made fun of them and said, 'They have had too much wine.'" [33] Peter's response - that his men were not drunk because "It's only nine in the morning" – is a somewhat unconvincing argument for temperance and leaves some lingering questions about their usual state later in the day, but we'll leave that as an unanswered aside to history.

It didn't take long for the mild indifference and cynical disdain of the majority of onlookers to turn into harsher criticism and then violent re-action. Not surprisingly the first response came from the Sadducees, that pseudo-religious sect which had evolved out of the misty years between

---

33   Acts 2:12,13

the Old and New Testaments. With the help of some priests and a contingent of the Temple Guard they managed to haul Peter and John off to jail for the night. The next morning they were summoned before the High Priest along with some of his family members and other religious officials. It should be noted that the Sadducees were resolute on one doctrine, that there is no resurrection. I apologize, but I have to resort to the little Sunday School adage, "That's why they were sad, you see."

Clearly the apostles had been preaching the resurrection, but they had also trusted its power by which they had healed a cripple who now, healed and healthy, walked in as a witness at their trial. [34] In the face of this evidence and in the presence of no great crime, the council released the two apostles with instructions to desist from preaching in the name of the One from whom they claimed their authority. Little did Peter know that his next words would launch countless millions of Christ's followers onto the path of 'justifiable civil disobedience,' a path that led many to martyrdom, as it does to this day.

"Judge for yourselves," Peter responded, "whether it is right in God's sight to obey you rather than God, for we cannot help speaking about what we have seen and heard." [35]

Within a matter of days – and only one chapter of the Book of Acts – Peter and John were 'at it' once more, preaching and healing the sick in the Name of Jesus. What else could they do? Again, they were brought before the temple authorities.

"We gave you strict orders not to teach in this name," said the High Priest.

"We must obey God rather than men!" replied the apostles; and the battle lines were drawn for all of history. [36]

---

34   Acts 4:1-21
35   Acts 4:19,20
36   Acts 5:26-29

Persecution continued and became more intense. Those opposing the new sect had a champion; a righteous zealot in the garb of a Pharisee, Saul of Tarsus. He "began to destroy the Church. Going from house to house, he dragged off men and women and put them in prison." [37] It was at this juncture that something magnificent took place; something against which I want us to compare our modern Church. The first verse of Acts, chapter eight tells us, "On that day a great persecution broke out against the Church at Jerusalem, and all except the apostles were scattered throughout Judea and Samaria."

Please note; the apostles were still in Jerusalem. The 'preachers' were not scattered abroad. The apostles, prophets, evangelists, pastors and teachers were still huddled around the table. Those who had the ability to draw the crowds, preach the Word and lay hands on the sick and raise the dead were still at home. Those who, if they came to our neighborhood would be ensconced in fine hotels, air lifted by helicopter into the nearest stadium to be met with rapturous applause by the waiting masses, those for whom we would line up for hours just to have hands laid on our heads by the 'man himself'; and for ever after be able to tell our grandchildren, "I was prayed for by Peter." All of those 'greats' stayed back in Jerusalem when the greatness of the Church was first displayed beyond its birthplace.

Verse four of that chapter, states, "Those who had been scattered preached the word wherever they went." The Church – the people – the members – were scattered, the Bible says, 'throughout Judea and Samaria,' but this is what impresses me; everywhere they went, they preached the gospel.

Amazingly, the Great Commission was taken from one quarter fulfillment to three-quarters in a matter of weeks as a result of the ministry of 'ordinary Church members.' Jesus had said, "You will receive power when the Holy Spirit comes on you; and you will be my witnesses in

---

37   Acts 8:3

Jerusalem, and in all Judea and Samaria, and to the ends of the earth."
[38] By the actions of ordinary folk, all that remained after their first
enforced outreach was, "the ends of the earth." But let's be clear about
this, the apostles were not lacking here. I am not implying that they
were the lazy ones left behind. By the power of the Holy Spirit they had
obviously equipped and infused the earliest members of the Church
with a passion and zeal for the gospel and a fiery concern for lost mankind; the same heart which they had received from Jesus Himself. And
this is where our next comparison must begin.

If the members of your Church were to be decimated and scattered to
the four winds, what would be the result? How would you compare to
the First Church of Jerusalem? Would there be a broadening of your
Church's sphere of influence or would the strength once felt in the
congregation disappear? Would it result in multiplication or drastic reduction? If you and your family suddenly found yourselves in a strange
country, a place in which you had not planned to live, among people
whose customs contrasted to your own values and preferences, would
your presence begin to change that culture or would you and your children be assimilated into the values of your new home?

Let me soften the blow a little! Everywhere the first Christians went
they would have found a type of people who might be rare in our
modern world. They do exist, but not as obviously as in the first century A.D. They could be described as "God fearing." Some already had
links to the Jewish faith. Jews numbered somewhere between 7 - 10%
of the population of the Roman Empire, including many of those new
Christians who were now being scattered. As a result of the scattering
from Jerusalem many of those returned to cities in which they had
grown up. Once there, they would find these "God fearing" citizens,
ready to consider what they had to say.

Those scattered Christians would have another advantage not enjoyed

---

38   Acts 1:8

by our generation. People in those days willingly attended any spectacle which presented itself for public viewing. Not so today! Right up until the 20th Century and the advent of the radio and television - which now keep families predominantly within the walls of their homes - any public assembly would not only draw the adherents of that group, but would also attract a crowd of interested observers. Even as late in history as the early years of my life, I recall Salvation Army bands marching along the main streets of English towns with several dozen people walking alongside to enjoy the music and the spectacle. This was recognized as a good way to get people 'into the meeting.' "Come, follow the band," was a well known saying and a productive strategy.

In earlier times, any form of gathering which involved debate, music, drama or any other expression which might transport the listener out of their everyday world and into another, would draw a healthy crowd. In 19th Century Albany, New York, the Shaker meetings, complete with music and dance as part of their worship, would provide multi-tiered bleachers on either side of the worship area for the general public to sit and observe the proceedings. It was a regular night-out for interested observers.

It was in the 1980s when we first began to speak – prophetically, it would seem – of people 'cocooning' themselves inside their homes, next to their television. Now, in the 21st Century, that piece of equipment has been elevated to become the outlet for the Internet, You Tube, and movies on demand. Impersonal communication with the outside world is on hand by means of texting, tweeting and Facebook, all of which will be laughably out-of-date within a few years. Surely this means we don't have the same opportunities to spread the gospel by drawing a crowd as would a first-century public meeting or even a twentieth-century Salvation Army Band. May we be excused because of this difference in the cultural setting, this contrast with the First Church, surrounded as they were by a population of prepared people, ready to hear the gospel? Did our first-generation Christians have an advantage over us which we cannot expect?

To be fair to these scattered first-century believers, they were no longer part of a group of several thousand, as they had been in Jerusalem. A crowd attracts a crowd, and their daily meetings back in the Temple Courts must have been a sight to behold, with thousands in attendance and hundreds more looking on; a real crowd pleasing spectacle! [39] However, after the scattering, they were probably numbered as individuals or small family units. Nevertheless, everywhere they went the gospel was preached and people were convicted, convinced and committed to the Savior of that little displaced alien remnant. Without doubt, they were a different breed to the modern Church member. Perhaps only a few contemporary believers might 'measure up'. It's not fair to generalize, you say, in every congregation there will be those who "gossip the gospel" wherever they go, and there are many who make a testimony by the simple expression of their personal wholesomeness. Their impressive moral health and even the absence of a foul mouth make a noticeable contrast with their fellow-workers. Yet generally, compared to those first Christians, are we the Silent Church?

The predominant spirit across much of the Western Christian community is often one of fear, or at least a concern not to be too noticeable. People who regularly witness to their faith are seen as 'a bit fanatical.' Perhaps they are 'new converts', and we expect them to 'grow out of it'. The depictions of Christians on popular television programs don't help the image. The only character depicted as a Christian in the 'Sopranos' series greeted everyone with, "Have you heard the good news?" Naturally, thinking themselves 'good Catholics', the Mafioso treated him as some sort of irrelevant fool; exactly what people would expect of an 'evangelical'. But is it entirely the fault of the screen writers? Would they have characterized him differently had they themselves been exposed to a healthy presentation of a life transformed by the

---

39   Acts 2:46

power of God? Did none of them grow up with friends who were sensible and effective Jesus people?

The Early Church was fleeing intense persecution, but many of my friends own up to simply not wanting to be ridiculed by people at work or in the classroom. Some first-generation Christians were ripped up by lions and set alight as human torches, but God forbid that we would ever be scarred by sarcasm or seared by the office cynic!

I sometimes think that our most common strategy for winning the world is to trust in what might be called 'evangelical osmosis'. As if by being close to the world - but not of it - is sufficient to transmit enough of the gospel to shake people to repentance. The really brave among us at least give an invitation to attend a meeting, but the majority has yet to even risk such confrontation. Their strategy for the Christian Church of the 21st Century is to expect people to magically appear in our meetings of their own volition or by the direct causation of the Holy Spirit. But if that were possible, don't you think He would cause everyone in town to turn up on Sunday morning? Do you seriously think there's anyone in your neighborhood that God doesn't want to save?

If the vast body of lost humankind is expected to hear the good news without it being told to them, then forget the Second Coming, Father. It looks like You'll have to delay it for a few more centuries. After all, Jesus did say, "This gospel of the kingdom will be preached in the whole world as a testimony to all nations, and *then* the end will come." [40] So if that "end" depends on our willingness to communicate the good news wherever we go, perhaps the end is yet a long way off?

The prophets of our generation have ached at the thought of the lost going through life without as much as a hint at the redemption found

---

40   Matthew 24:14

in Christ. Sometimes their words are cutting and too close for comfort. Keith Green wrote,

Open up, open up, and give yourself away,
You've seen the need, you hear the cry, so how can you delay,
God's calling and you're the one, but like Jonah you run,
He's told you to speak, but you keep holding it in,
Oh, can't you see it's such a sin?
The world is sleeping in the dark
And the Church can't fight, 'cause it's asleep in the light,
How can you be so dead, when you've been so well fed?
Jesus rose from the grave, and you, you can't even get out of bed. [41]

---

41   From "Asleep in The Light" by Keith Green

Life Group Discussion
Chapter 3: The Silent Church

We have an amazing example set for us by the members of that first Church who were persecuted and scattered, and yet as refugees and aliens they changed the society wherever they went. This chapter asks some difficult questions. Let's face up to them and give our answers.

Questions for Discussion

1. Bill asked, "*If the members of your Church were to be decimated and scattered to the four winds, what would be the result? Would there be a broadening of its sphere of influence or would the strength once felt in the congregation disappear? Would it result in multiplication or drastic reduction?*"

2. The U.S. Army has used the slogan, "An Army of One." We suppose this to mean that all the qualities that make up a great fighting force are to be found in each individual warrior. What qualities do you think were lodged in the individual members of the Church of Jerusalem that resulted in them being so effective even when they were separated from the main body?

3. If people really are 'cocooned' in their homes more than in earlier generations, how can your Church interact with them?

4. Do you find yourself thinking that our goal is to "get them to a meeting"? Was this the aim of the scattered believers? If not, then how do you think they were so successful? How do imagine they did it, if not through meetings?

THE SILENT CHURCH

Jesus, Your are the Shepherd of the lost.
You didn't come for the ninety-nine alone, but for each individual —
especially the last lost 'one'.
We want Your heart, Your motivation, Your vision for those around us
who have yet to know of your amazing grace.

4

A Church by Any Other Name

When Jesus said, "On this rock I will build my Church and the gates of Hades will not overcome it," [42] how come He used the word *Church* when there was no such thing? Why didn't the disciples say, "Build His *what?*" We all know the Church was birthed on the Day of Pentecost fifty days after Jesus gave Himself as the Passover sacrifice. So why did He use a term which was yet to be put into common use? Or did He?

The answer is simple. He used the word *ekklesia*; a word *everyone* understood. He said, "Upon this rock I will build my *ekklesia*." We can safely assume that's the word He intended and we may also assume He knew what it meant. However, we English speakers have possibly adorned, or more accurately, 'undressed' that word. *Ekklesia* meant so much more to the disciples and others alive in Jesus' day than that which we attribute to *Church*.

So here we go with more comparisons! Does the word, "Church" hold the same significance to us as did the word Ekklesia to the first Christians? You decide... Let's compare our contemporary understanding to that of the first-generation. Did *Ekklesia* mean attending

---

42   Matthew 16:18

meetings, belonging to a congregation, joining in worship? Or, while including all of those elements, did it mean so much more?

The worst definition of 'church' might be found in a dreadful musical I wrote, many years ago as an angry young man. As Bob Dylan said, "I was so much older then; I'm younger than that now."

> *The Church is an abbey with a big studded door,*
> *A stained glass window and a stone cold floor,*
> *The Church is a Bingo hall, a furniture store,*
> *The Church is a building – The Church is a bore.*
> *The Church is a steeple – an echo of tune,*
> *A Poster for Christmas, still hanging in June,*
> *The Church is a font – The Church is a tomb,*
> *The Church is "Prepare to Meet Thy Doom."*
> *The Church is a bell on a hot summer's day,*
> *A man with much speaking and little to say,*
> *The Church is for keeping your conscience at bay,*
> *And old people's music, without a DJ.*

Ekklesia is one of three words in the New Testament which need to come into play here. When you consider these three, perhaps you'll agree we have mixed them up somewhat, but their real meanings strike right at the heart of what the Church is all about. Let's begin by going back to that conversation between Jesus and His disciples; the one when He said, "Upon this rock." The rock of which Jesus spoke was the revelation, given by the Father, about who Jesus was and is and ever shall be. Many people have tried to make this about who Peter was, but the actual context is about the identity of Jesus. That was the point of the conversation.

On a couple of occasions I have been asked to participate in a forum involving a Jewish scholar, a Muslim Imam, a Roman Catholic Priest and me. It was a public forum, and I was asked by the moderator to open the proceedings. Usually the opening speaker at these events seeks to establish some common ground from which the rest of the event can grow, so that's exactly what I did. "This is our common ground," I began. "Our commonality begins and ends at our individual response to one simple question. Jesus asked it of His disciples and, one day, I believe each one of us will hear Him ask it once more. How we respond to His question will determine where and how we spend eternity. The question He will ask is this; 'And who do you say that I am?'"

In response to that question, Peter said, "You are the Christ, the Son of the living God." [43] That was the revelation upon which Jesus said He would build His *ekklesia;* upon the revelation of His true identity.

To get a better idea of why Jesus used that word, *ekklesia*, we need first to take a look at the other two words in our vocabulary threesome. One is *kuriakos*, and the other, *sunagoge*. That last one is easy to translate; it sounds a lot like 'synagogue'. In fact, it has the same meaning. *Sunagoge* was the Greek word for an assembly, a gathering. We would call it 'a meeting'. Let's face it, take away the *sunagoge* – the meetings - from most contemporary Western World Christians and there would be precious little left! To 'make it to the meeting' is a major challenge for 21st century believers. Gone are the days when attendance at a Church meeting was a 'given'. Now, across the United States at least, it is a commonly held position among pastors that if you want to say something to your congregation, you'd better spread it over several weeks. Seldom, if ever, will you get the entire membership together in one place, at one time.

I was born into a Salvation Army family, and boy, did we do *meetings!* Our Sunday schedule went something like this....

10:00am   Children's Sunday School – adults out on the streets at an open-air meeting

---

43   Matthew 16:16

11:00am   The Holiness Meting – the entire family in attendance. Yes, kids actually sat and listened to the sermon!

2:00pm   Children in Sunday School – Adults once more out on the streets

3:00pm   The Praise Meeting – again, the whole family in attendance.

6:00pm   The entire church is out at an open-air meeting in some nearby neighborhood, children included.

7:00pm   The Salvation Meeting, a lively mix of music and praise followed by a salvation message… and the kids, having previously attended morning and afternoon Bible classes, now hear their third sermon of the day!

8:30pm   The "Wind-up" – an informal praise and testimony time to conclude a full and busy day. Hardly the 'day of rest'!

Add to that, Tuesday evening Choir Practice (for kids and then adults) - Wednesday evening band practice (again, kids first, then adults) – Thursday evening Bible Class and Friday Youth Club. Saturday was often spent at a special Church festival or concert. And the rest of the week was our own!

We kids had a special little book we carried to Sunday School. Although it contained Bible memory verses, songs and choruses, we called it our Star Card because attendance at Sunday morning and afternoon sessions got us two stars on the register page. If we were legitimately sick and unable to attend, a note from home got us an "S" in that week's space, and it counted as a full star. If, while on vacation, we attended Sunday School in the resort town we visited we got an "H", for Holiday. A full register of attendance, for all fifty-two weeks, morning and afternoon, gave a total of one hundred and four stars and I cannot recall ever receiving less than that, all the years of my childhood until, at the age of fourteen, I graduated into the adult Church as a fully trained soldier of Christ! In a nutshell, if the doors of our Church were open, we were there. We did 'meetings'!

That was then, and as they say, this is now. Modern families could not possibly maintain a schedule like that even if they wanted to. The main reason, among others, is that we're all too busy! I'm not convinced we do any more than families did in the 1950s, but we are much, much busier than they ever were! Our lives are crammed with all the *essentials* of what it takes to exist in our modern world and making it to a worship service is often crowded down on the list of priorities. God understands, we tell ourselves, even if the pastor doesn't!

Fortunately, however, Jesus did not say 'upon this rock I will build my meetings'. But suggest that to your average Church member nowadays and he might adopt it as the best excuse yet for staying in bed on Sunday morning. I have nothing against meetings; I love them, most of the time. I love the Body of Christ getting together. I believe regular Celebration with the entire congregation is absolutely essential to a healthy life in Christ. How can we be the Army of God if we're not 'on the same page,' hearing, saying and singing the same thing? The Celebration get-together – whenever it is held – holds all those 'same page' elements in a way that no other expression of Church-life can offer.

The first Church in Jerusalem definitely had meetings, of all shapes and sizes. "They devoted themselves to the apostles' teaching." [44] We know that they assembled themselves regularly. "Every day they continued to meet together in the temple courts" and the apostles went from there to make the rounds of their homes. "They broke bread in their homes and ate together" [45] and, "in the temple courts and from house to house, they never stopped teaching and proclaiming the good news that Jesus is the Christ." [46] Did you see that? It said, "Every day" they had meetings, and yet they also belonged to a home-based Life Group? Who *were* these people!

---

44   Acts 2:42
45   Acts 2:46
46   Acts 5:42

Justin Martyr, a scholar and writer who lived in Palestine in the early second century, described early Christian meetings this way: "On the day called the Day of the Sun all who lived in cities and the country gather together in one place." So the early Christians certainly enjoyed their meetings. They were – and are – a natural expression and outcome of a group of people who share the same vision and values. But for them - those first believers - attendance at a meeting would never have been seen as the end of the matter. People don't get martyred for meetings! There are no *sunagoge saints*!

So if *sunagoge* stands for meetings and gatherings and we admit that real Church is more than that, then what about the second word on our list? Funnily enough, it's the least known of the three and yet it's the one most closely linked with our English word, 'church'. It is *kuriakos*. This word means 'that which belongs to the Lord.' This is the root for the English word, *'church'*. Take *kuriakos* and give it to the ancient Germans and *kirihha* comes along. Let it loose among the Norse invaders and it will sound like *kirke*. Listen to it as spoken by the Picts and the Scots, who had a Christian community long before there was an England, and they shorten it to Kirk (as they do to this day). Of course the English had to get in on this; of old they called it *cirice* and, eventually, *church*. But the word simply made the point that every believer belonged to the Lord. After all, we are not our own, we were bought with a price. [47]

That brings us to our third word, *ekklesia,* the one translated throughout the New Testament as 'church'. So here is yet another comparison. Does our modern concept of church compare favorably with the understanding the early Christians had about the word, ekklesia, or do we - who admit to being kuriakos - still languish back in sunagoge?

To find the answer we must discover *ekklesia* in its historical context. By the time Jesus used that word it had been in common use for hundreds

---

47   1 Corinthians 6:20

of years. It had little or nothing to do with religion. If anything it was a governmental term thought up by the Greeks. In the development of their concepts of democracy, they came upon the idea of appointing certain people from within a community to stand as representatives not only of the needs and challenges of that community, but also the values of the government as relating to their local community. These people were literally *called out* from their community to represent their kingdom. That was quite a privilege and no small responsibility!

The Romans had a way of borrowing ideas from Greek culture; anything they thought worthy or useful. They ruled with an iron fist but they had the wisdom to show tolerance and flexibility whenever possible, and they weren't averse to adopting ideas and strategies from others, especially from the sophisticated Greeks. Greek culture, they believed, gave legitimacy to their empire's identity in ways that brutality and military power might never quite achieve. And so, in Roman Palestine and throughout the Roman world, the ruling authority adopted the policy of appointing a *called out* group of citizens through whom they would seek to establish the values of their kingdom. Their word for this group was the Greek term, starting with *ek*, which refers to a place out of which one comes, then the word, *kaleo*, which is the root of our word *call*. The *ekklesia* is a group of *called out* citizens.

It could be inferred that these people, in the Christian sense, were simply being called out to a gathering – to a meeting. But if that's the case – if that's what Jesus had in mind when He spoke of the building He was about to construct – why not just say, "Upon this rock I'm going to call a meeting; I'm starting a new synagogue."

Over the years, the word church has come to mean, primarily, the building occupied by Christians when they have their meetings, or it can refer to the actual meeting itself. What a travesty! At least in recent years we have heard clear teaching which is rooted in the principles of the New Testament, that the Church, the ekklesia, is the people. Now, however, we need to move one step farther. We are not just people who are *called out* of the world, *called out* of our old lifestyles; we are primarily *called out* to be called into a position, purpose and authority. We are Christ's Ekklesia – representatives of His kingdom - called to enact the authority of His realm in the midst of the earthly community. "On earth, as it is in Heaven."

There are times in our meetings which we recognize as being 'anointed,' blessed with a special sense of purpose and presence. The proclamation of the Word has a prophetic edge to it and the music of praise rises beyond the ability of the musicians. Bondages are broken, in bodies and souls. Eyes of understanding are opened, and hearts released. Earthbound humans join in worship, in spirit and truth, and something is changed in the heavenlies surrounding the place where they meet. These are the times when the Church touches its position and function of ekklesia, even when still in sunagoge. We are especially in our ekklesia calling when we are in warfare, intercession and when we are winning souls. We are ekklesia when, like the prophet Nathan, sitting beside his king and holding him accountable, we speak boldly to earthly governments. The Christian women of Liberia were ekklesia when they faced their tyrannical president, Charles Taylor, demanding an end to the years of civil war. Those women may still be poor, but they are free, and Mr. Taylor is condemned to 50 years in prison! Whenever we are fulfilling the actual purposes for the Church on earth, then that is ekklesia. Everything else is merely a rehearsal.

Life Group Discussion
Chapter 4: A Church by Any Other Name

In this chapter, three words are featured, each of which has something to do with our understanding of the Church. Let's start our Life Group by identifying their meanings,

Kuriakos   _____

Sunagoge   _____

Ekklesia   _____

Questions for discussion

1. Given a correct understanding of the word *Kuriakos,* is it possible to be regular at the sunagoge, but know nothing of kuriakos? What does Matthew 7:22, 23 have to say in that regard?

2. Let's make a list of the various ways by which we might fulfill the purpose of the Church on earth. Then, let's ask this question: *If you were making a chart to gauge the amounts of time and energy spent by your congregation on all its various Church activities, which activity has the highest rating?*

"Does our modern concept of church compare favorably with the understanding the early Christians had about the word, ekklesia, or do we - who admit to being kuriakos - still languish back in sunagoge?" Let's spend some time discussing this question. Let's look for creative answers. If necessary, we must ask the Holy Spirit to change our priorities and values.

Lord God, we don't want to organize Your Church around our interests, neither do we want only to be involved with what we can see and touch. We want to serve Your purposes and fulfill our mission here on earth by taking our place of authority over the seen and unseen enemies of mankind. Empower us, Holy Spirit, to stand as Your Ekklesia!

5

Are We the Mob or Are We Members?

It's interesting to read the account of the Church's early days in Ephesus. This was a city of great influence and significance in the earliest ages of the Church, eventually housing the third ecumenical council in 431 A.D. and another, highly controversial council in 449. Well before those days, however, Ephesus became known for the attention given to it by Paul in one of his greatest epistles. We are all familiar with Paul's letter to the Ephesians. The fourth chapter of that letter has helped us understand how Jesus, at His ascension, released the offices and gifts of His own Person to the Church. "But to each one of us grace has been given as Christ apportioned it. This is why it says: "When he ascended on high, he led captives in his train and gave gifts to men." … It was he who gave some to be apostles, some to be prophets, some to be evangelists, and some to be pastors and teachers, to prepare God's people for works of service." [48]

At first sight Ephesus didn't seem to attract much attention from the apostle. He called in on the way to a handful of other cities. At least he left Priscilla and Aquila behind to follow up on a brief visit he had made to a local synagogue. A gifted scholar and teacher named Apollos also called in and showed real promise for the gospel, so Priscilla and

---

48   Ephesians 4:7-12

Aquila mentored him for a while before sending him on to Achaia. [49]

Eventually – inevitably - the rubber met the road! Ephesus was the center of a major religion of that day. Artemis was held to be one of the greatest of Greek gods. Some believed she was the daughter of Zeus himself, so although the news of the One True God and His Son went down well with the local citizenry it did not with those who lived by the one false god and his daughter! This was especially the case with those who profited from the temple of Artemis and the many silversmiths who made a good living selling objects of worship.

A man named Demetrius, a silversmith, made an angry trade union speech. "You see and hear how this fellow Paul has convinced and led astray large numbers of people here in Ephesus and in practically the whole province of Asia. He says that man-made gods are no gods at all. There is danger not only that our trade will lose its good name, but also that the temple of the great goddess Artemis will be discredited, and the goddess herself, who is worshiped throughout the province of Asia and the world, will be robbed of her divine majesty." [50]

You'll notice the gospel had not only attacked the religion of the locals, it had also interrupted their business, and *that's* serious! A crowd formed, shouting "Great is Artemis of the Ephesians!" And soon the whole city was in an uproar. But the crowd was little more than a mob. Some shouted one thing and others yelled something else. There was no cohesive voice, no agreement or unity of purpose and consequently no legitimacy or genuine authority. [51]

Exciting as this tale is in its own right, and much as I love telling the stories of the New Testament for their own worth, let me reveal why I'm relating this story to you; it's because of what happened next. The city clerk stood before the crowd and remonstrated with them for their

---

49   Acts 18:24-28
50   Acts 19:25-27
51   Acts 19:32

behavior. "Men of Ephesus….If, then, Demetrius and his fellow crafts-men have a grievance against anybody, the courts are open and there are proconsuls. They can press charges. If there is anything further you want to bring up, it must be settled in a legal *assembly*. As it is, we are in danger of being charged with rioting because of today's events…"

There it was; Greco/Roman government; Pax Romana, with a slice of Greek culture thrown in. "If there is anything further you want to bring up, it must be settled in a legal *assembly*." Literally, "*a legal ekkle-sia*". "As it is," the clerk said, "we are in danger of being charged with rioting." The clerk reminded them that if the citizenry form a crowd by any other means but by the authority of the government, they are little more than a mob. However, if they are called out to enact a legitimate expression of the government then they would be recognized as a legal *ekklesia* in the historical sense of the word. A crowd without authority is a mob.

In the modern church we like crowds. If a preacher can draw a crowd we assume he or she has authority. Surely a large crowd is a sign of God's blessing? If a pastor draws only a small following it might be a sign that he's unimaginative and not too gifted, but is the opposite always true? Is the size of the crowd a sure sign of true anointing? Do large crowds only gather where the ministry people have godly dignity and proven character? The truth is; the largest crowds often have little discernment in such matters. Crowds follow signs and popularity breeds popularity, and popularity is seen as success. The bigger the crowd we assume the bigger the "Church". If a man can attract a crowd then he will be given a seat among the elite. He will be asked to represent the kingdom. The world, in the form of CNN and others who see popularity as great-ness and anoint it with celebrity, will ask the preacher who draws a crowd what his views are on this or that contemporary subject. In our naiveté we express disappointment when the preacher who draws the largest crowds appears vacuous in the face of questions from the media. Perhaps we assumed that large arenas would only be served by the Billy

Grahams of this world, with all his attendant dignity and godly character, but we would be wrong. Large crowds are no sign of legitimacy. In
the world of popular culture the mob has authority because popularity
is the ultimate sign of legitimacy.

Not so in the kingdom of God. Jesus said, "Woe to you when all men
speak well of you, for that is how their fathers treated the false prophets." [52]

I don't have anything against large crowds gathering to hear the gospel. In the earliest years of my ministry I regularly spoke to thousands
'live' every week and several million more on television. However, I
recognized before I was in my mid-twenties that the larger the crowd
the easier they were to control. I find little difficulty speaking to a vast
crowd. It's far more challenging trying to convince an individual, going
'one-on-one'. And when it comes to assessing the 'size' of a congregation, coming from a rural area of New York State I must insist on the
introduction of a caveat. Let the size of the crowd be assessed in rela-
tion to the size of the population of the surrounding area.

When Pastor Jim Cymbala of the famous (and sizable) Brooklyn
Tabernacle was asked how he kept himself from pride, he responded that several thousand people attending his Church only served to
remind him that there are 2.6 million people in his surrounding bor-
ough and 8.2 million living in the city. Add to that the 54.2 million
visitors that enter the city each year and you have a fair picture of the
context of his "crowd". A congregation of 10,000 in a city of 8 million represents 0.125% of the population. That's six times smaller than
the representation our congregation has in our surrounding area. But
our Church is "small" because, in the Church, crowds are only "large"
when compared with other congregations. We seldom take the brave
step of comparing them with populations!

---

52   Luke 6:26

Every step away from a person's individuality is a step away from accountability. It's far too easy to hide in a crowd. I would go as far as stating that the size of the crowd in the Church is often commensurate to the level of discipleship required of the members. Is that true? If a Church leader demands more from his congregation, deeper commitment, evident discipleship, active involvement, personal accountability, actual response, will he be rewarded with larger crowds, or smaller?

Do I admire Bill Hybels? Let me count the ways! However, what most impressed me was when he confessed that many of the things that attracted tens of thousands to Willow Creek Church were the very things that allowed too many of those thousands to remain ambivalent to the gospel, or at least apathetic toward discipleship. He said, "We made a mistake. What we should have done when people crossed the line of faith [to] become Christians, we should have started telling people and teaching people that they have to take responsibility to become 'self feeders.' We should have gotten people, taught people, how to read their Bible between service, how to do the spiritual practices much more aggressively on their own." I think what he meant was 'How to be ekklesia and not just sunagoge!'

I heard Hybels preaching to one of those vast crowds one Saturday evening. I loved every minute of it. He pulled no punches. But it was all too easy to "relax, turn off your mind and float down stream," too easy to trust in 'Christianity by osmosis'. But as the old preachers used to say, "You can sit in a garage for years but that doesn't make you a car." Nothing was demanded of me at Willow Creek, nor was it of any of the other ten thousand people in the place. We didn't sing, pray or outwardly worship; it was all done for us and done excellently! I'm sure many attended and lived for Christ, but so many others were allowed to sit and watch the show, then go home, having done their bit for Jesus. That may have touched *sunagoge* but they were nowhere near *ekklesia*.

In the Western Church we are close to practicing ochlocracy. [53] Close, but not quite! We don't actually allow the *rule* of the masses, but we are sorely tempted to make Church as attractive as possible to as many people as possible. Really successful Church plants these days must begin with a vast budget, part of which is spent well before the first publicity goes out about actual services. It is spent assessing the "felt need" of the culture in the chosen region. When they gauge that 'felt need' they can direct their emphasis, set their themes and establish their priorities in order to attract the largest crowd. So tell me, who's in charge here, the Holy Spirit, the Church staff, or the crowd which has yet to attend the first meeting?

In his writing on 'Democracy in America,' Alexis de Toqueville spoke of the danger of the tyranny of the majority. In a democratic society the infallibility of an opinion is proved (or improved) by the numbers of people who hold it. Popularity is evidence of being right. So democracy is only morally productive when the majority of the people *are* right, so it will probably work in Heaven, but by then we will all have happily surrendered our rights to the One who *is* right. Right?

An acquaintance of mine recently left a smaller congregation, attracted by a larger publicity-heavy, seeker-friendly, weekly-on-TV, unthreateningly-edgy, shaggy uncombed haircut, single tuft mini-beard on lower lip, tight jacket and cuffs over the fingers, props on the stage for the sermon, right off the freeway, 'church'. She sat there for some months until one Saturday evening she looked around.
"The masses," she said. "They crowded in. Then it hit me. It's just like professional wrestling. It's all staged, even fake, *but everyone acts like it's real.*"
But man, was it popular.... And costly! Such activities will never be sponsored by bank loans and few venture capitalists will show interest, so we can only imagine a 'Mega-church' elsewhere is the sponsor of this level of mass media marketing - a crowd giving birth to a crowd. But

---

53   Ochlocracy = Government by the masses; mob rule.

the formation of a crowd is one thing; building a Church is another. Getting the two confused is a matter of life and death for the Church, especially because a large crowd will look like success and will propel its leaders into prominence. The actual death may be delayed until the Head of The Church has something to say about it.

The earliest believers could not possibly have been crowd oriented. Everything was so painfully personal. To be a follower of The Way [54] – which was the name adopted by the first-generation of believers who had yet to be called *Christianos* [55] - they understood the words of Jesus when He said, "If anyone would come after me, he must deny himself and take up his cross and follow me. For whoever wants to save his life will lose it, but whoever loses his life for me will find it." [56] And, "If anyone comes to me and does not hate his father and mother, his wife and children, his brothers and sisters — yes, even his own life — he cannot be my disciple. And anyone who does not carry his cross and follow me cannot be my disciple." [57] Not exactly a populist position. Maybe Jesus didn't have the right marketing strategists!

First-generation Christians knew the sting of separation from the comfort of popularity, although, as we've seen, adoption into the family of the Church held compensatory comforts. Eventually it meant outright persecution. The word *martyr* originally meant *witness;* those who were willing to witness to their faith, at any cost. They were described this way: "They overcame him by the blood of the Lamb and by the word of their testimony; they did not love their lives so much as to shrink from death." [58] And that word 'testimony' is from the same root as *martyr.* Anyone for a time of testimony? Let's go 'witnessing'!

---

54   Acts 9:2
55   Acts 11:26
56   Matthew 16:24-26
57   Luke 14:26,27
58   Revelation 12:11

Life Group Discussion
Chapter 5: Are We the Mob or Are We Members?

In this chapter a clear distinction is made between a crowd – a gathering – and an ekklesia, a legitimate, representative, authoritative body of people.

Questions for discussion

1. What can transform a crowd into a genuine ekklesia? Is it something that the leaders do, or the people in the crowd, or a combination of both? What is the difference between the gathering of a crowd and a Church?

2. Church planter, author and pastor, Bill Hybels made a powerful statement quoted in this chapter. What were the elements he wished had been more forcefully built into the early years of his Church?

3. Large crowds and popularity have accompanied Billy Graham throughout his long ministry career and yet he always stayed on track. What qualities do you think God found in him to make this possible?

4. In a culture that rewards popularity, what are the dangers that accompany the leaders of small Churches which largely go unnoticed by the media? This is important, because half the Churches in North America have 75 members or less. [59]

In this chapter we read, *"Every step away from a person's individuality is a step away from accountability. It's far too easy to hide in a crowd."*

---

59   Ref: http://www.internetmonk.com/archive/michael-bell-what-is-an-average-church

We have a dual challenge; to see our congregation grow and to see each member grow up as a true disciple of Jesus. How can we ensure that our 'crowd' does not become a hiding place for those who don't want personal accountability?

Lord, help us to never hide in the crowd.
However large or small our congregation may be,
help us to see that we are all individual members in Your Body.
Teach us never to satisfy ourselves in the size of our crowd,
but only to be fulfilled by our individual obedience to You.
and help us to spur on those around us to genuine discipleship.

6

Limbs and Body Parts

Jesus told Peter and the rest of His disciples that He was about to build a called-out expression of His government; His Ekklesia. This would be far more than a *sunagoge*, where communities of like-minded people would gather to pray, sing, read from the Law and the prophets and plan family and fellowship. In an Ekklesia those precious qualities would simply be complimentary to its governing purpose. Every member of an Ekklesia would be an ambassador. Whether they were called to represent the local governor's latest edict or declare a new law from the emperor himself, they came together for a high purpose. They stood out from their communities while at the same time representing them, like intercessors, standing in the gap, having hands in both camps. [60]

Now Jesus was calling out His Ekklesia, the Church. "We are therefore Christ's ambassadors," Paul wrote, "as though God were making his appeal through us. We implore you on Christ's behalf: Be reconciled to God." [61] But before we can assume ambassadorship we must be taken through a process. First we are called out from our old place, as part of a lost crowd. Peter wrote, "[God] called you out of darkness into

---

60   Ezekiel 22:30
61   2 Corinthians 5:20,21

his wonderful light. Once you were not a people, but now you are the people of God." [62] So before we become ambassadors we are initially called out from the crowd, out of our old position. However, ambassadorship is not just a case of what we're called out of - it's also what and who we are called into! We are called *out* of the crowd and *into* Christ. Then we can stand as His Ekklesia, to do business for His kingdom. We are not merely called to be part of a new crowd, exchanging one mob for another; we are called to be *members* of Christ.

The difference between being part of a crowd and enjoying membership would appear to be obvious. However, in our generation of Church life the latter has been demoted to be synonymous with the former. To understand this we need to imagine ourselves back in the first century.

At the time of the birth of the Church a person's position in this world was determined by the circumstances of class, creed and culture. Into whatever class they were born, as a ruler, an aristocrat, as a person in the military, a merchant, a serf or a slave; that was their lot in life. Very few ever made the transition from one level to another. Indeed, despite its generations of Christian influence, this was still the case in Europe until the days of Jane Austen and Charles Dickens! Modern day India is struggling with this very same burden as it seeks to climb out of the darkness of its cast-ridden past into leadership in the modern world. But two thousand years before, long before these social struggles, the class mold was broken by the birth of the Church.

A man called Celcus was a harsh critic of the Church in the first century. He was not bashful to describe the motley crew of Christianity in these terms: "Far from us," say the Christians, "be any man possessed of any culture or wisdom or judgment; their aim is to convince only worthless and contemptible people, idiots, slaves, poor women and children... These are the only ones they manage to turn into believers."

---

62   1 Peter 2:9,10

From his perspective, he had a point. He had never seen such a mixed bag of culture all claiming oneness and community. By no means was the Church solely made up of the uneducated masses, but it certainly gave voice, identity and place to those who otherwise would have been completely disenfranchised by their lowly background. Membership was open to whosoever!

When we think of membership we usually have an idea similar to joining a golf club or a local gym. You pay your dues and sign up. The exclusivity factor is usually determined by the cost of joining, relative to other clubs. If you have the prerequisite cash, you're in. This, of course, was impossible in earlier times. Now and then great wealth might somehow buy position. A Roman general and even an emperor or two were known to come from humble beginnings - the spoils of war can do wonders for the bank account - but the class system usually held. So what did the Church mean when it spoke of a membership, open to all-comers?

Let's look at this word, *member*. Doing so, from a biblical point of view, opens up an entirely new world. Not only will we see the revolutionary changes that Church membership brought to the society it touched, but it should also shake the flimsy foundations of most of our ideas of Church membership in our day.

First, let me ask you a question: Why do you think it hurts so much when someone leaves your Church? I hope it *does* hurt. It should! Gather any group of pastors around a table — and I sit with the usual suspects every week, meeting for prayer and breakfast with the leaders of Adirondack Churches Together [63] - and hear them speak of those knife wounds so carelessly inflicted by departing "members".

It's not just a case of diminishing statistics or being considered a failure in the ministry. It goes much deeper than that. If it were merely

---

63   See "adkchurches.com"

members leaving the local gym it would just free up more exercise equipment for the rest of us; their loss! But Church membership is a different matter. People might say, "Don't take it so personally" when someone leaves. But how can you *not* take it personally, they're committing the act of amputation, and it's my body they're playing with, but more importantly, it's Christ's!

That's true. The New Testament word for 'member' is *melos*. It means 'limb' or 'body part'. Back to those Ephesians again; Paul told them, "Therefore each of you must put off falsehood and speak truthfully to his neighbor, for we are all members of one body." [64] To the Corinthians, Paul jumps from describing the human body to the Church Body. "God has combined the members of the body and has given greater honor to the parts that lacked it, so that there should be no division in the body, but that its parts should have equal concern for each other. If one part suffers, every part suffers with it; if one part is honored, every part rejoices with it." [65]

You put your hand to your head when your head is aching because the other part of the body brings relief, not just because the hand needs something to do! They are complimentary parts of one body. "If one part suffers, every part suffers with it." That's because in the Church we are not just a crowd, a mob; we are body parts. Paul goes deeper: "We will in all things grow up into him who is the Head, that is, Christ. From Him the whole body, joined and held together by every supporting ligament, grows and builds itself up in love, as each part does its work." [66]

We have already considered the incredible depth of commitment that Early Church members had for one another. They sold their homes, took people in, cared for the poor and the widows among them, to

---

64   Ephesians 4:25
65   1 Corinthians 12:24-26
66   Ephesians 4:15,16

the point that no-one among them was in need. The emperor Julian [67] complained to his governors, "Atheism *(This is how Romans referred to Christians; those who didn't follow the Roman gods)* has been especially advanced through the loving service rendered to strangers.... The god-less Galileans *(Christians)* care not only for their own poor but for ours as well; while those who belong to us look in vain for help."

Even the growth of the Church was linked to this concept of every person in the community being a body-part, a functioning limb, con-tributing from its own strength to the overall health of the body. Paul wrote, "The whole body, joined and held together by every supporting ligament, grows and builds itself up in love, as each part does its work." [68] A literal translation would say, *"The growth of the body makes for building of itself."* There is a name for a cell within a body which ceases to perform properly; it's called Cancer.

When you think of Church growth, what comes to mind? Is it the individual working of every member, or do you expect it to come from some marketing strategy, the reputation of your preacher, the style of your services or the offering of multiple time slots in which they will be conveniently held? Maybe you trust in the excellence of your worship band. What causes growth? In Paul's words, it's "the proper working of each individual part."

It's not just in leaving a Church that we show a less-than-stellar under-standing of membership, it's also in the joining of a Church. Paul said, "The body is a unit, though it is made up of many parts; and though all its parts are many, they form one body. So it is with Christ, for we were all baptized by one Spirit into one body." [69] This verse says that we are placed into the Body of Christ by the Holy Spirit. So how do you think He does it? Does He have a box of new-born limbs that He just throws in the general direction of the body, or do you think He has a strategic

---

67   Roman Emperor Julian – A.D. 332-363
68   Ephesians 4:16
69   1 Corinthians 12:12,13

placement for each limb? Will He put a nose here, an arm there, and hope they somehow combine to become a healthy unit? That may be Picasso's method, but not God's. Or will He place us according to His desire to bring encouragement and strength to our annexed limbs and glory to Jesus, the Head of the body?

If you join a Church indiscriminately, in the same off-hand manner that many leave, you are not rightly discerning the Body of Christ. Here in Queensbury, New York, when we organize "Welcome to The Family" classes for prospective members of Church of The King, we begin by stating that the classes are not recruitment sessions. We announce, "We believe everyone has a place in the Body of Christ. We believe in the placement of the Holy Spirit, so we are committed to help you find that place. If it isn't here, then we will do all we can to help you find where it is."

I have found that people can adhere to a congregation for the oddest reasons, many of which are anything but healthy. Some have unresolved issues with the "last place" where somebody offended them, so they walked down the street and carried their offense into another part of the Body of Christ. Given that understanding of membership it's just like sowing a wounded limb onto a healthy body. Good luck with that!

Others choose their congregations as one chooses a supermarket. All the shelves are in the right place, the price is right and they like the ease with which they can make their way in and out with the minimum of inconvenience. Also, it's open at times which suit their busy schedule. However, should someone from *corporate* come in with a new layout which inconveniences the old familiarity of the place, they vote with their feet. There's always another supermarket down the street!

I recently spoke to a young lady who had been rudely reprimanded by one of her sisters in the faith. She was offended and left our congregation. I sat with her, in tears.

"You're like family." I said, my voice broken with emotion. Tears flowed down her cheeks, too. "Don't you see how this is hurting so many people who have laid down their lives for you?"

She did, but it didn't seem to matter. In her understanding of how Church works her offense was justifiable and outweighed the fact that she was cutting off a valuable limb. She was dislocating and amputating herself from the rest of us, leaving us weaker in the process. There are no winners here! And the pastor who welcomed her in to her new *membership* is actually welcoming an open sore into his body!

The writer of Proverbs said, "A brother (or a sister) offended is harder to be won than a strong city: and their contentions are like the bars of a castle." [70]

We've already established that Church life is so much more than attending a meeting. However, the writer of Hebrews says, "Let us not give up meeting together, as some are in the habit of doing, but let us encourage one another." [71] So, amazing as it seems, even our meetings are not just for us, for our edification or entertainment. By simply attending a meeting we become an encouragement to other body-parts. Conversely, by dislocating ourselves, whether by leaving the congregation or simply by staying home, we become an active discouragement. How could it be otherwise? We are limbs placed together; active joints, muscles and sinews "joined and held together by every supporting ligament." [72]

Paul rightly assumes that a healthy person will take care of his own body. "No-one ever hated his own body, but he feeds and cares for it, just as Christ does the Church—for we are members of his body." [73] I'm encouraged to hear that Christ cares for His Body, the Church, and

---

70   Proverbs 18:19
71   Hebrews 10:25
72   Ephesians 4:16
73   Ephesians 5:29-31

He calls us to care for and nurture our fellow members in like manner. "We know what real love is because Christ gave up his life for us. And so we also ought to give up our lives for our Christian brothers and sisters." [74] And so we should, they are limbs on our body.

---

74 1 John 3:16 (New Living Translation)

Life Group Discussion
Chapter 6: Limbs and Body Parts

"Membership" – we participate in all sorts of activities through it: the PTA, the 'Y', a supporters' club, a homeowners' association. But membership of Christ's Body is altogether different, especially when we understand the biblical meaning of the word.

Questions for Discussion

1. What is the meaning of the Greek word, *Melos,* which we translate as 'member'?

2. Given that meaning, how should we approach choosing which Church we should be joined to?

To a certain degree the true meaning of membership has been lost in translation since New Testament days. First-generation believers didn't 'translate' biblical terms as we do. They knew and understood them to mean what they literally were. So they thought themselves to be 'body parts' - 'limbs'.

3. In what ways do you think this understanding affected how they regarded and treated each other?

4. When someone leaves a congregation and removes themselves to another part of the Church, across town, what does our understanding of *melos* suggest is actually happening? What are the full effects of this action?

As Paul said, "No-one ever hated his own body, but he feeds and cares for it, just as Christ does the Church—for we are members of his body." Let's close this session by spending some time expressing our appreciation for acts of love and care which have affected our lives.

Lord Jesus, we have thought little of Your Body, the Church. We have carelessly inflicted wounds and neglected to heal open sores. Help us to care more for one another and teach us to be more sensitive to the value and placement of each part of the Body of Christ.

7

Man's Hand in God's Business

Implicit in anything made by man are the seeds of its downfall. We build our structures, plan our strategies, erect our monuments and launch our movements, hoping they will hide or at least compensate for our foibles. But time and circumstance have a way of summoning our hidden weaknesses to the surface, for all to see, and for history to record.

This is never more the case than when the hands of men take hold of that which only Christ can build. Like Uzzah, reaching out to save the Ark of the Covenant from falling by the wayside, we stretch beyond our office and ability to wrest the church from some impediment, only to reshape her in our own damaged image. [75]

The innocence of the Early Church did not last long. The challenge of sustaining a spiritual kingdom in the midst of a pagan and secular world was as real for the first Christians as it is for us today, the main difference being that their Church was young and vibrant, fresh and clean; ours has needed countless restorations and revivals to allow us even a hint of the original.

---

75   2 Samuel 6:6-7

When did things begin to change? It began almost as soon as the last apostle left this earth to inhabit his promised inheritance in Christ. The greatest challenge to any group of people who have encountered God in some special way is how to communicate the wonder of that season to those who are hearing it second-hand. The problem for second generation members is that they are, to one degree or another, living on the faith of their forebears. And that is never enough! Just as the Old Testament is rife with heroes of the faith who toiled to bring about restoration to Israel and Judah, so the Church has required the same breed; those who live in the present but whose hearts are still rooted in the original and whose eyes are looking beyond their horizon to what no man has yet seen. These prophetic figures cannot stand the stench of compromise or the comfort of lethargy and inertia which comes by way of bequeathed faith.

To be fair to this second-generation of Christians, they had not enjoyed the personal encounter that gave birth to the Church. Many of them had been born into faith; born, that is, of the insufficiency of the flesh.

The freshness and enthusiasm of the first days of the Church began to fade during the second century. Not that the Church was shrinking, on the contrary it was exploding until every outpost of the Roman Empire had some evidence of a Christian community in its midst. But, as we have already seen, crowds and popularity are not the stuff of God's kingdom. Only that which is born of the Spirit, alive in the Spirit, and led by the Spirit, is relevant.

First-century believers had done such a good job that Christians were becoming a recognized slice of the social pie by the time of the second century and the outcome led to the Church becoming secularized. There were always those, of course, who tried to bring revival and life back to the drying bones of Church life. One such man was Montanus. He appeared on the scene like a voice in the wilderness, crying out like John the Baptist for the Church to repent and regain its place of discipleship, holiness and separation from the world. Unfortunately Montanus and the revivalists he influenced did not stay close to the authority of the Word. He insisted that the Old Testament had been surpassed by the new age of the Holy Spirit. Even Jesus was relegated to a secondary place.

The Church's response to this was to begin the process of establishing the canon [76] of scripture; a process that was long, complicated and to this day, disputed. But correcting doctrine was not the only challenge facing the second century Christian community. People who have little understanding of the ways of God will always revert to the ways of the world. At first the Church had come out of the world, fleeing the evils of the surrounding society, but as we all know, when you stop fleeing, that from which you have fled has a tendency to catch up. The Church's biggest challenge was now to decide what to do with those inside the Church whose lives were hardly discernible from those outside.

In earlier days it had been clear. The apostles planted Churches and appointed pastoral leaders for the flock to draw it on to fresh pasture. Those leaders were called elders; the original New Testament word was *presbuteros* which had its roots in the idea of being *elderly*, but age was not the qualification, there was an assumption of other more spiritual qualities.

In the Acts of the Apostles we read, "Paul and Barnabas appointed elders for them in each Church and, with prayer and fasting, committed them to the Lord." [77] Paul instructed Titus, "The reason I left you in Crete was that you might straighten out what was left unfinished and appoint elders in every town, as I directed you." [78] The duties of those early elders were much the same as in many Churches today. They would teach new converts, arrange meetings, lead public events and take care of disciplinary matters. Paul instructed Timothy, "The elders

---

76   The word canon originally meant rule or measuring stick
77   Acts 14:23
78   Titus 1:5

who direct the affairs of the Church well are worthy of double honor, especially those whose work is preaching and teaching." [79]

But power is a seductive ingredient to the soup of character. It is so often mistakenly assumed that the person with the most influence should be given the most power. But power should only be the outcome of proper authority which involves a two-way street of intrusive accountability, leaving no man as an island. Without accountability power is seldom constructive, and its user can easily lose sight of his own fallibility.

The Church in Antioch was a creative apostolic community. It was there that the followers of the Way were first called Christians, [80] and it was to that church that Barnabas brought Saul. It was probably in that 'naming place' that Saul was first called by his Greco/Roman name, Paul. And it was in that same Church, in the next century, that a leader called Ignatius sent letters out to the Churches referring to a single leader, using a word which had been used in apostolic times but was about to assume a position not previously occupied. That word was *episkopus,* meaning overseer or bishop.

The idea of this single pastoral leader slowly gained acceptance around the Christian world. The bishop began to sit as the leader among leaders in the eldership, the deacons making up a third tier of leadership. To the same degree as the position and power of the bishop was defined so the actual Church (the people) began to recede.

Naturally, the responsibility to counter the heresies attacking the Church fell to these men. They became the voice beyond all other voices, not only in conversations about doctrine but also in the matter of the recognition of Church membership. It didn't take long, however, before the inevitable took place and the bishop, as head of the

79   1 Timothy 5:17
80   Acts 11:25

Church, became identified even with the forgiveness of sin and a person's membership in the kingdom of God. If the bishop said a prodigal was reaccepted, he was, - kill the fatted calf. If a person, whether prince or pauper, had some question about his salvation, it was not a certainty until the bishop said so.

When we consider the effect of the super-spiritual and ecstatic ravings of the Montanists we can understand why the Church needed educated apologists to counter heresy, but the prevailing culture had increasingly set a fixed gulf between the uneducated serf and the landed and lorded ecclesiastical gentry. How could "the people" – the actual Body of Christ – be trusted to deal with heresy? And they were not the last generation to think that it needed a professional elite to have the academic sophistication to even discern between wrong and right. The church was changing.

At the same time as the authority of the overseer was being defined, the Church was struggling with its acceptance by secular society. Trying to fit the gospel to the culture of the time is not a new invention. Just as in our day, communicating with the contemporary culture often led to compromise and accommodation rather than revolution, and the result was often new doctrines which challenged the Church's foundations.

A new breed of Church leaders was born out the need to refute these unsound doctrines – and there were plenty of those around in the years following the last apostle's death. They were called *apologists*. This sounds as if they were apologetic for their beliefs, but in fact the word means that they were attempting to make a reasoned defense. This is not easy when the aim of the apology is the jaded world of Greek philosophy. The pressure to be recognized and accepted by the sophisticates of the academic world can lead Christian scholars to try to work a synthesis between God's Word and the philosophies. Sometimes this worked – some of the philosophers were sincerely doing their best to find answers to life. A few actually made some sense! But any attempt to appease a sophisticated world can fall foul of denying the simplicity of God's kingdom – the principles of which can be understood by those whom Jesus referred to when He said, "I tell you the truth, anyone who will not receive the kingdom of God like a little child will never enter it." [81]

Not only might the Christian scholar become embarrassed by the simplicities of the kingdom, he might also begin to feel shame for the simple people attracted by the kingdom's gospel. At first the presence of simple working class people was celebrated. Athenagorus was a philosopher in Athens who wrote, "Among us are uneducated folk, artisans and old women who are utterly unable to describe the doctrines in words, but who attest them by their deeds." But such grace was not always extended to the more simple-hearted among Christ's followers.

It was necessary for early Christian leaders to speak to all levels of the prevailing culture, just as it is in our generation. There is no segment of society which does not need to hear of their possible redemption and their certain judgment. The problem comes when attempts to engage the more sophisticated parts of society become mixed with the desire to be accepted, even admired by them. At that point we must ask who is leading the conversation and who is converting whom?

The persecution of the Early Church knew no social boundaries. Governors and generals, teachers and lawyers, stood shoulder to shoulder in martyrdom with peasants and slaves. To the lions they all tasted the same and to the watching crowds their testimony – their martyrdom – was equally eloquent. But as those days passed and the Church gained a hold on the highest rungs of the social ladder a separation took place between the common and the elite in Christian society, eventually leading to a distinction between the educated priest and the lowly laity.

---

81   Luke 18:17

The early Christians had been persuaded by Peter himself that they were "like living stones…being built into a spiritual house to be a holy priesthood, offering spiritual sacrifices acceptable to God through Jesus Christ." [82] This meant that even the lowliest task of the slave could be done to God's glory as a sacrifice of praise; the slave or the Centurion could be a priest. By the second century, however, lowly tasks were lowly; more *spiritual* service was desired, honored and admired and became the province of a higher class and a better breed.

In earlier times the witness of the martyrs had elevated them in the minds of their contemporaries to a higher plain. Eventually their birthdays were recalled and celebrated in their memory. However, as their generation passed away these 'saints' were joined by another enthroned hierarchy as mystics and monks withdrew to their caves and bishops retired to their palaces. The lowly believer who pushed a plough was now neither saint nor priest.

Three hundred years after the resurrection of Christ the world had been transformed by the Christian Church. Constantine, the emperor of Rome in the early 4th Century, made a move against a rival who had superior military power. Constantine claims to have seen a vision of a cross in the sky as he heard the words, "In this sign conquer." He advanced on his foe and won the day. Convinced that the God of the Christians had taken his side he was gratefully converted. From that time on the progress of Christianity throughout the known world was inevitable, not now through the personal response of an individual to the work of the Holy Spirit, but by the power of man's hand, especially when it held a Roman sword.

Forty years after the emperor's conversion Augustine was born in what we now call Algeria, on the North African Mediterranean coast. Among his writings, beloved by Roman Catholics and Baptists alike, he added his considerable weight to the idea of the priesthood, as distinct to the

---

82   1 Peter 2:4-6

so-called laity. A group called the Donatists claimed that the moral standing of the priest was significant to his ministry, especially in the act of administering Communion. Augustine disagreed, stating that the sacrament did not belong to the priest, but to Christ. The priest, then, he claimed, became a channel of God's grace – literally a *means of grace* – to the people. Perhaps inadvertently, Augustine allowed the Church to travel from the innocence of those who had known but one mediator between God and man; the man Christ Jesus, [83] a journey they would continue avidly!

Considering these steps away from the Church's earliest simplicity it is not hard to believe that bishops became lords and princes, literally holding in their hands and at their discretion the eternal destiny of all from the slave to the king. Excommunication was the Bishop's greatest weapon. To be sent out from the Church was to be banished from all earthly society and any heavenly hope, simply because the bishop said so.

The Bishops of the generations following the birth of the Church soon held life and death, heaven and hell within their hands. Granting not only access to heaven, they also calculated the price sufficient to free a living person or their deceased relatives out of Purgatory and into the heavenly realm. Never mind our contemporary congregations – if Paul had walked in on Augustine's Church, would he have known where he was?

---

83   1 Timothy 2:5

Life Group Discussion
Chapter 7: Man's Hand in God's Business

The challenge of handing on the baton from one generation to another is fraught with difficulties and the Early Church was not immune from that struggle. Let's begin our discussion by reading the first two paragraphs of this chapter.

Questions for Discussion

1. In what ways do you think we might reshape the Church in our own image? Why is this a tendency?

2. There has always been a 'first among equals,' right back to the Jerusalem Church when James took a leadership position in a dispute between Peter and Paul, so what started to go wrong with the emphasis of one leader (Overseer or Bishop) in the Early Church?

3. The Church began with a clear understanding of the priesthood of all believers and that all the redeemed are 'saints'. How did it happen that the priest began to be a separate and higher position, and how did the "Saints" become so revered, at the expense of the everyday believer?

4. What can we do to restore the place of the priesthood of all believers in our congregation?

5. During this period the Church grew "not now through the personal response of an individual to the work of the Holy Spirit, but by the power of man's hand, especially when it held a sword." What is the fundamental problem with this kind of Church growth?

8

Schisms and Divisions

When God looks down on your city, how many Churches does He see? How many Churches were there in Jerusalem? When Jesus revealed His message to the seven Churches named in Revelation, how many cities were involved? Were they the seven Churches on the Lower East Side of Ephesus? Maybe there were seven Churches in the suburbs of Smyrna or Downtown Pergamum. No, it would appear that the seven Churches were named for seven cities, one in each.

The unity, the oneness of the Church in its earliest years is evident. The apostles started their ministry together, in one place and in one mind. That is not to say they didn't have to work hard to maintain that unity. Paul purposely used the word *spoudazo,* which is a root word for our idea of speed when he said, "speed up – hurry along – don't delay – the unity of the spirit," [84] fully implying that it is all too easy to slow the process down with pettiness and personal preferences. So what happened between that era of unity and the present diversity we now see? Is unity impossible when God's kingdom on earth grows beyond a certain point? Is diversity necessarily the enemy of unity? Once more we need to take a brief walk through history.

---

84   Ephesians 4:3

To begin we must understand that during the first centuries of the Church the world was not made up of nations as we now know them. We cannot refer to people by their national identity as much as we might by their clan or tribe or under which warlike ruler they found themselves. Some of these tribes were nomadic, so for these people 'their land' meant the place where they presently lived or had recently and successfully invaded rather than some beloved real estate which had belonged to their forefathers from time immemorial.

The conversion of the Roman emperor Constantine eventually imposed Christianity upon the entire empire which stretched from the Irish Sea to northern Sudan. Salvation, as taught by the apostles, was replaced by a form of Christianization, no longer a personal response to the tug of the Holy Spirit, it became something political, cultural, enforced, even bullied. It was a very effective way to add numbers to the baptismal roll; "Repent or die!" The grandchildren of the martyrs had turned the tables!

A hundred years later Augustine penned his epic, 'City of God' and although he attempted to draw mankind's attention away from temporal cities – especially apt at a time soon after Rome had been sacked by the Goths – and toward God's City in the heavens, the idea of a city of God on earth was too tempting for the princes of the Church that followed. 'Christendom' was born; a territorial kingdom won over not by the persuasion of the preacher but by the sword of the victor. The vanquished became the convert, if he was lucky.

The kingdom of the Franks was to become deeply significant when one of their kings would eventually become the first Holy Roman Emperor. But that kingdom's first foray into Christendom was bizarre and typical of the times. Clovis, the founder of the nation, was having a tough time on the battlefield. Like Constantine, his Roman predecessor, he cried out to the God of the Christians for help. "Give me victory and I will be baptized." Whether he won the battle by superior strategy, the sun getting in his opponents' eyes, or by the fact that his enemies had eaten bad pork the night before, we will never know, but like Constantine before him, victory came and he attributed it to God's intervention. The local bishop was summoned and Clovis was baptized. I can't find any record of baptismal classes or a discipleship course before the event but he and three thousand of his soldiers were added to the roll that is presumably called up yonder. Whether they liked it or not, and whether God liked it or not, they were all now "Christians".

These mass conversions, although entirely alien to the reality of true salvation, were the way in which hundreds of thousands came to be known as Christian. The great unifying element of Christendom was built throughout Europe. The Church had become catholic, coming from the Greek word *katholikos*, which originally meant "on the whole" or "in general". But this earthly government - inflicted and coerced by armies and princes claiming the mandate of Heaven - now united the church as 'Catholic.'

Pax Romana had covered much of what we would call 'the known world' but as the old empire came under attack from Vandals and Goths from the north and the Huns from the east it became a tattered array of its old self. One factor remained over the empire's vast domain, the influence of its Christianization; an influence which eventually won over most of the pagan invaders. The world into which the Church was born was being reshaped and prepared for the future and the Church was being remade in the process. She was being conformed to the pattern of this world rather than transformed into that which is good and pleasing to God. [85] Not for the last time, the Church was being converted by that which it was called to transform.

Amazing as it may appear, throughout these turbulent generations there were always those who stayed close to the purity of the Early Church. Whether in a desert cave, a monastery, or even in the offices

---

85   Romans 12:2

of an ecclesiastical prince, never was there a total absence of those who knew that their hearts had been quickened by the breath of Him who breathed on His disciples, saying, "Receive the Holy Spirit," [86] but they were a remnant, a minority, a precious few.

In generation after generation the name of Jesus was used and abused for the most evil and destructive of purposes. We would readily place such evil at the feet of the world's despots and dictators such as Stalin or Hitler but as much blame belongs on the records of those who claimed to be acting for the kingdom of God and the Prince of Peace. The attacks of the Vandals and Goths were met with a desperate and furious response by Christian armies as the invaders tore into the realm of the Church's empire. The first millennium seemed to be filled with equal amounts of blood and doctrine as Christian armies slogged and slugged their way through tribe after tribe, "Christianizing" as they went.

That challenge of Paul, to "Make every effort to keep the unity of the Spirit through the bond of peace," [87] is the only ground for unity; that which is laid down by the Holy Spirit of truth and that which is the free choice of the participants. Unity in the Church based on anything else is a sham, a pretence, at best a dream, but throughout Church history bishops, princes and popes have imposed their own brutal brand of coercive control, and called it 'unity'.

But only that which God builds will last. After writing, "For no one can lay any foundation other than the one already laid, which is Jesus Christ," Paul continues, "If any man builds on this foundation using gold, silver, costly stones, wood, hay or straw, his work will be shown for what it is, because the Day will bring it to light. It will be revealed with fire, and the fire will test the quality of each man's work. If what he has built survives, he will receive his reward. If it is burned up, he will suffer loss; he himself will be saved, but only as one escaping through

---

86 John 20:22
87 Ephesians 4:3

the flames." [88] Great monumental parts of this façade still stand today. Spiritually speaking it was and is a building of wood, hay and straw but it was literally built with seemingly immovable marble, political power and intrigue; all of which will fall on that Day of Fire, if not before.

The monstrosity of early Christendom could not exist forever without godly men and women crying out their dissent. But their voices were yet to be heard. Divisions of other sorts tore at the fabric of Christendom. Pride, jealousy and power can never produce anything but a perversion of unity. Church splits these days are often about such 'major' things as someone feeling ignored or offended by another member or, worse still, by the pastor. The splits in earlier days tended to be about doctrine. We at least have most of our doctrine sorted out. It's just our behavior that is lacking.

The first great split came by way of what appeared to be a great unifying factor, the conversion of the emperor Constantine. He hoped to bring unity to the church by giving it a legitimacy and profile at a governmental level, but even more he hoped to unify his far-flung empire by the introduction of Christianity to every citizen. He moved his capital from Rome to the empire's eastern province. The ancient Greek city of Byzantium became Constantine's headquarters. He called it Nova Roma but it became known as Constantinople – Constantine City.

At the time this must have looked like a wise strategic move. Just like the modern city of Istanbul - the city's name after the Muslim takeover in more recent history - Constantinople sat like a gate - even a revolving door - between east and west. But the creation of this eastern capital sowed the seeds of not only the empire's eventual division but also the Church's first great schism.

The seeds of this split lay under the soil of the definition of sin and salvation. Salvation is the most basic and essential of Christian beliefs.

---

88   1 Corinthians 3:11-15

Outside of true salvation there is no such thing as a Christian and no such thing as the Church. A clear understanding of true biblical salvation had already been all but lost, so it is not surprising that Church leaders, separated as they now were in East and West, Rome and Constantinople, further muddied the waters.

In the West, ideas of sin and salvation came through the Church. The Roman priesthood, with the *Pontifex Maximus*, the Highest Priest between Heaven and Earth, was in place. Sinners sinned – as was their tendency - and the Church, through the office of the priest, determined the severity of the sin. This judgment call then determined the cost of the recompense owed to God to attain forgiveness and salvation; a price conveniently payable to the local priest on behalf of the Almighty! If the sin happened to be too costly for the earthly wealth of the client then Purgatory awaited him where he could 'work-off' the residue of his debt; a compelling strategy which I envy for its ability to keep any congregation in regular attendance!

In the East, sin was seen in a different light. It was considered to be a corruption of the divine image, the *icon* of divinity in human creation. [89] The use of icons remains to this day. They are seen as objects not only of worship but of actual communication from God as clearly inspired as the Holy Scriptures. On these and other issues the Church of the east and west had their differences.

In the course of all doctrinal disputes personalities clash and egos vie for the upper hand. Reputations are at stake, and that's enough for any philosophy to be left back at the starting blocks of the race. The clash between East and West came to the boil by the beginning of the second millennium when Cardinal Humbert, a representative of the Romans, paid a visit to the great Church in Constantinople in order to make a contribution. He marched up to the altar, but he was not about to make a friendly donation to the building fund. His deposit

---

89   Icon = the Greek term for image.

was a declaration of excommunication for the Eastern Church. The first great schism had begun.

In New Testament times salvation was seen as the result of a personal encounter between God and an individual. It was offered to all, whatever their station in life. The unity of the Church came through the individual choice to glorify Jesus, call Him Lord and choose, every day, to live in harmony and agreement with fellow believers. Then, salvation became something found only in the Church, whose princes guarded it as strictly as they did their crowns, rings and jeweled chalices. And like the crowns and jewels, it could be purchased – at a price.

In the meantime, princes and popes alike continued with the idea that Christianity could be spread abroad by brute force and conquest. Crusaders, carrying the cross of Jesus on their chests and shields did not represent us well as they raped, pillaged and murdered every Jew and Muslim in their path, as they made their way to win back Palestine and the Holy City from the hand of the infidel. Just how holy the streets of Jerusalem remained as those blood-soaked warriors entered her gates – and few succeeded in doing so - is open to debate.

In the 1970s Lynn Green was the national director for Youth With A Mission in the U.K. His heart for God's kingdom and his understanding of Church history was obvious when he heard the call to organize 'Reconciliation Marches' from Western Europe, following the routes of the Crusades. He told me that more than once he and his team were met with the same response from Imams and Muslim community leaders, "We have no problem with Jesus; it's the Church we hate." To the American school child, 1492 was the year when "Columbus sailed the ocean blue," and all of Europe turned westward. Islam, however, recalls that year as the time when the last remnant of their hold on Europe was pushed out of Andalusia and back into the Mediterranean. Europe, facing west, forgot that Islam was over their shoulder and Muslim memories are long.

Many of the knights, princes and kings who gathered their armies for those grim pilgrimages which we call the Crusades (and after which we blindly name our choirs and school sports teams) did so as a response to the princes of the Church who sold indulgences in order to fund these campaigns. Indulgences were also sold to sponsor the erection of some of Europe's finest cathedrals, not the least being St. Peter's Basilica in Rome. An indulgence is the "full or partial remission of the punishment due for sins". The belief is founded in the idea that a treasury of excess righteousness has been deposited by the saints – originally, the martyrs – which can be drawn upon, at a price, by those less virtuous. That price could be anything from the mere action of viewing an icon – conveniently located in a bishop's palace – all the way up to vast fortunes paid for the erection of a cathedral or the funding of a crusade.

This concept belongs to the reckless belief that salvation can be obtained by righteous works; a belief which revolted priests such as Luther and other leaders of the Reformation. At first, however, Luther was not openly opposed to indulgences but when his contemporary, John Tetzel, coined the rhyme, "A coin in the coffer rings, a soul from purgatory springs," Luther's better angels – which were not always in attendance - gained the upper hand, and his destiny was set.

As a reaction to these and other beliefs, men and women were, once more, willing to make their witness - their martyred testimony – and stand for the purity of the gospel at the cost of their lives. Reformation and counter-reformation were accompanied by the Inquisition. The sins of that era are too many and too gross to contemplate. I have visited one port city in northern Colombia where the Inquisition raged for 300 years. A small grille is mounted on the outer wall of the main torture chamber – now a museum – where citizens had only to write the name of a person – no charge; no evidence - and place it in this little cage, and that person would be dragged off to the inquisitors to meet certain, slow and painful death.

Considering the presence of worthy followers of Christ in the midst of the foul soup of what the Church had become it is not surprising that more cracks of division would appear which would eventually grow into chasms. Was the Body of Christ – the One Church of the New Testament age - being torn apart, or could the unity of the Body of Him who is its Head still remain, somewhere in the sweat and blood of this confusion?

Life Group Discussion
Chapter 8: Schisms and Divisions

In his book, 'CHOICES', Bill makes this statement:

"In order to grant us these attributes which make up this wonderful capacity to relate, God took what we might think was an almighty risk; He set His humans entirely and totally free, because He knew there was no such thing as a meaningful relationship without it being in the context of absolute freedom of choice. God also understands that no quality of character can be formed without that same freedom. Choice is at the root of everything worthwhile, but it can also be the doorway to every form of foolishness. Choice, unhindered, unfettered, without manipulation or control, is the hub of relationship."

And yet Bill states in this chapter, *"The progress of Christianity throughout the known world was inevitable, not now through the personal response of an individual to the work of the Holy Spirit, but by the power of man's hand, especially when it held a sword."*

Questions for Discussion

1. Why is it impossible to enjoy a genuine relationship through coercion or control?

2. *"No quality of character can be formed without... freedom."* Why are loyalty, bravery and similar attributes worth nothing if the person was forced to comply?

3. If an entire army was conquered and then baptized, were they 'Christian'?

4. Have you ever found yourself trying to control others in order to get them to do what is right? How did that work for you?

"Church splits these days are often about such 'major' things as someone feeling ignored or offended by another member or, worse still, by the pastor. The splits in earlier days tended to be about doctrine. We at least have most of our doctrine sorted out. It's just our behavior that is lacking."

5. When someone is offended by another member of the congregation, what does Jesus say is the best way to begin the process of healing? (See Matthew 18:15-17)

"An indulgence is the "full or partial remission of the punishment due for sins". The belief is founded in the idea that a treasury of excess righteousness has been deposited by the saints – originally, the martyrs – which can be drawn upon, at a price, by those less virtuous."

6. Can we make a payment to work off our sin? Or perhaps we could do enough good deeds to balance out the bad stuff. Believe it or not, some Bible believing Christians *(is there another kind?)* live like this. Read Ephesians 2:8-10 and suggest to each other how you would answer someone who trusts in his good works for his salvation?

9

The Mosaic

Look closely at any mosaic and you'll probably see only a blotch of orange or a smidge of turquoise. Step back and the bigger picture emerges.

When we look at the modern Church – especially when searching for unity – we tend to look at our piece of the mosaic, usually decrying the lack of unity shown by all the other pieces toward our particular little smidge of the picture. Let's step back a bit.

I never thought I would lay down an argument in defense of denominations, but my position – historically at least - has modified somewhat. I continue to have a deep concern about the lack of genuine communication and basic Christian love between the various parts of the Church and I have a particular loathing for what might be called 'denominationalism'. Just as there is a difference between patriotism - the love of one's own nation and its people – and nationalism, which is a regard for one's own people at the expense and to the degrading of all others, so there is a difference between the denominations and denominational-ism.

To appreciate how and why denominations appeared we must first celebrate one great feature of our created make-up; our freedom. My reading of scripture tells me that we are endowed by our Maker with a complete freedom of the will. This is what makes relationships possible. Without this freedom we have no ability to form character or even respond to God's call to repent. Freedom is the basis for personal responsibility. God is a just God. He will judge us on how we have used or abused our freedom, not on what He caused us to do by the imposition of His sovereign will. Let the causer be judged! [90] It is this position of freedom that sparked the Reformation, although some of its heroes still insisted on the Augustinian concept that God's sovereignty causes all things – good and bad.

As dogged disciples of Augustine, the concept of tolerating another's differences would have been an anathema to Martin Luther, John Calvin or Loyola of the Jesuits. They were made of a different cloth. They allowed no doctrinal basis for the freedom of the will, so they had little or no need to consider tolerance for another person's point of view. All they saw was the other person's wrongness and they believed their position had been predetermined and sovereignly established by God. Another person's disagreement with their position must, therefore, have been similarly established by God's sovereignty. Kill them, torture them or drown them, it mattered little, they were obviously already doomed. That, in the extreme, is *denominationalism.* Modern-day proponents don't kill each other, but tolerance is a dirty word and grace and mercy were long ago drowned, strapped to the ducking-stool of doctrine.

Recognition of the freedom to choose - the personal responsibility of every individual on earth - gives rise to a greater understanding of grace. Another person's denominational or doctrinal viewpoint is not an affront to my own; it is merely that person's expression of their God-given freedom for which they will be held responsible before God. That doesn't mean I won't attempt to express my view or even encourage my

---

90   This is the theme of Bill's book, "Choices – Stop Blaming God."

brothers and sisters toward my position, but I'll try to do so lovingly and with respect.

Predictably, the Roman Catholic Church as well as many early Reformers resisted the idea of free choice when it came to an expression of faith. This was not only because of their belief in God's sovereign causation of all things, but also because the Christian Faith had become the national, collective identity of any people-group. The identity of the individual was still subservient to the community, or at least to the governors of that community. Great cities had grown into principalities and the princes gained their authority, as well as their personal salvation, from the princes of the Church. Give citizens freedom and the authority and dominion of those princes in their castles and cathedrals might come under greater scrutiny.

From Medieval times and on into the age of the Reformation, city-states were identified by their doctrinal position. Many a Reformation thinker was banished from his city only to run to a neighboring region where his beliefs were tolerated. Soon this "running" took people even farther afield in their search for freedom, from France, Italy and England, into the Low Countries and even across the Atlantic to the New World. These pioneers were all but stateless. Their search for personal and religious freedom had led them to the fringes of the authority of the old despots back home.

At first, even in the New World, conformity was still the status quo and banishment and excommunication were the answers to those who didn't fit the mold. But if a free thinking citizen of Massachusetts was banished out into the wilderness, at least he (or she) could make a short journey to a neighboring settlement where greater tolerance was offered. In some of the colonies in the New World the bishops of the Old World still held their sway, insisting that the rights of citizenship only belonged to those who were members in good standing of the State Church.

Gradually, citizens of Europe and the New World were unshackled. One-time illiterate and mute followers of a local priest who had been separated from God's Word were becoming schooled in the scriptures and consequently aware of their 'rights', not only in society, but more importantly, before God. Any sign of an affront to that freedom could not be tolerated and the denominations began to form. Freedom has a way of emerging into the light of day, even from blankets woven with the heaviest strands of conformity, especially if it is the freedom of the Holy Spirit.

The partitioning of the Church into its various denominations was often contentious and remains so to this day, but it was the stuff of freedom which is a gift of God to His creation. It was also the same spirit that gave birth to the basics of modern democracy. So I'm viewing the denominations not as a sign of division but of diversity; a natural outcome of God-given liberty.

The struggle for freedom of conscience and belief does not stop within the confines of a denomination. The climb out of the dark pit of coercion and control continues to this day. The old Churches of medieval times are still with us – although reshaped to a certain degree - with the addition of numerous offspring in the form of the denominations. Add to that mix the succeeding generations of non-denominational churches and we find ourselves surrounded by multiple listings in the local Yellow Pages identifying the names, addresses and cool web sites of the 'Churches' in our city. We can speculate who would remain on the list if Paul were to run his finger down the column and examine the doctrinal position and practices of each 'Church'. Perhaps some of the new additions would receive his encouragement and affirmation, whereas some who call themselves *orthodox,* he would classify as anything but!

Are we expected to see unity among all the shades of what calls itself the Church? The answer is simple: Not at all! There are certain basics, foundational truths, which are the essential identity of the Church and its members and therefore form the only ground for unity.

The first – and most essential - is that we must be born again. Were it not so serious it would be laughable to hear members of congregations who claim orthodoxy and authority say, "Oh, you're not one of those born-again-ers, are you!" One television priest recently preached on being baptized as an infant into the Church, then being 'born again' into Heaven upon death. I can almost feel Paul's blood pressure rising.

It would be a grave sin to tell people there is no Hell below us and above us only sky, or even to imagine such a thing. But the greater sin would be to admit the existence of God, Hell and Heaven, but to delude people into thinking they are saved by some means other than that which God recognizes. It is on this singular basis that I place the only hope for Christian unity. It's simple. Unless a person has been born in their spirit, by the Holy Spirit, they are still under the curse of the spiritual death which entered the human race after Adam's sin. God had warned that Adam would surely die if he chose disobedience. His physical body remained for many years, but his spirit died immediately. Since then, every one of his kind has been born spiritually dead, in need of regeneration. Outside of that re-birth not one Christian exists. Where there is no rebirth there is no Church, however long they have insisted on their legitimacy, however big a crowd they may draw to their rituals and however large and rich their altars may be. The New Birth and its accompanying new spiritual body constitute the essential space suit for life in Heaven. Without it, a person evaporates into Hell.

So when Christ Jesus looks down upon our planet, what does He see? He sees two people-groups. The first is 'the lost', aptly named because they don't know the Way. Jesus said, "I am the way." [91] If you don't know Jesus, you don't know the Way. You're lost. Then He sees the Church; and those who are alive in Him, belonging to Him, walking in Him,

---

91   John 14:6

and relating in love to one another. His Church is made up of those who: "have been born again, not of perishable seed, but … through the living and enduring word of God." [92] He spoke to His Father about these people, not only those whom God had given Him during His time on earth but, "also those who will believe in me through their message, that all of them may be one, Father, just as you are in me and I am in you. May they also be in us so that the world may believe that you have sent me." [93]

Those verses show how many Churches God has on earth; one. They also show that the world will be impressed by the unity of that Church, even believing that Jesus is from the Father by witnessing and experiencing the oneness of believers. We already know that the world is anything but impressed by our present and past disunity!

I am writing from my home region, the foothills of The Adirondack Mountains, two hundred miles (and an entire universe) north of New York City. Our Church history has been one of hard plowing on rocky ground. Revivals, Churches on every corner, Christian friends at work; they are all stuff of 'elsewhere'. The Mid-West or the Deep South with their Bible Belt mentality may as well be on another planet to our spiritual back yard.

When helping plant a Church in Richmond, Virginia, a friend and I visited a local school to see whether we could use some rooms for our first meetings. The principal met us and showed us round the property, starting in a room which would seat around fifty people.

"You could start in here and then, as you grow, you could move up to a larger room and so on, until you need to use the auditorium," she said, with a warm smile. She then led us to the dining room where two hundred kids were snacking out of their lunch pails. She called for silence.

---

92   1 Peter 1:23
93   John 17:20-22

"Children," she began, "these two gentlemen are starting a new Church. So, when y'all get home this afternoon, tell your parents that a new Church is opening in our school, isn't that great!" The kids seemed to think it was!

My mind went blank. I had been living in New York State for some years by then and I recalled requesting permission to use a school room for a Christmas drama night in our home town of Queensbury.

"Who is it for?" asked the teacher.

"We are a Church…" I began to say, but was interrupted by the sight of the teacher recoiling in what looked like acute shock. She literally jumped back away from me.

"Oh, no! You can't do that!" she stuttered. I don't think I could have shocked her half as much had I brought along a cattle prod.

A local bank refused us the use of a Community Room in our little city of Glens Falls with the excuse, "Well, we do have some federally insured loans…" Ah, yes, "The Separation of Church and State!" Being a transplanted Brit I sometimes forget the not-so-subtle denial of liberty that this little phrase has spawned, at least in our neck of the American woods. We are, after all, only a few miles from the least churched state in the Union, beautiful but alien Vermont. In my experience, our 'sweet land of liberty' has often shown herself less friendly to the gospel than dear old socialist Europe, by far!

The prevailing spirit of the Adirondacks has been independence and self-sufficiency which has hardly aided the unity of the Church. Yet in the midst of this we have witnessed a refreshing chain of events. It began soon after my wife, Jean, and I invited long time friends of ours, Roger and Doreen Brown, to leave their home and ministry in the UK, travel to New York and help us launch Church of The King. It was the mid 1990s. We had been in The Adirondacks since the late 1970s. It had been a hard slog but we had seen some changes for the better.

Roger and Doreen worked alongside us for the first few years of the new Church then set out on a state-wide prayer walk, all of three hundred miles from the Canadian border in Niagara to Queensbury! At about the same time they were both instrumental in arranging times of prayer and friendship between local pastors – and Adirondack Churches Together was born.

For the last fifteen years, a group of pastors has met for prayer each week, each man taking turns to host the event and a breakfast after the praying is done. At each location we pray not only for the ministry of that church but also for the pastor, his family, his needs, hopes and dreams.

We pastors had all participated in ministers' fellowships, often called 'clergy associations' of one kind or another and none of us were overly keen to repeat the experience. Although professionally cordial, the end product tended to be a guarded affair, with lighthearted banter about doctrinal differences and comparisons of congregational statistics which one group called the "*minijavs*" (How many did you have?")

The early months passed and our professional cordiality evaporated gradually, to be replaced by genuine friendship. In his role as coordinator of ACT, Roger Brown organized our involvement in the Global Day of Prayer, an annual event originating in South Africa which has spread across the globe. Pentecost Sunday is the day and date and we considered meeting – all of us, together with our congregations – in one place.

For me, that hardly demanded a moment's consideration. If it sounds like something God would do, that's enough for me and I knew my buddies in eldership and the family of the congregation would jump at the opportunity – at least after a healthy casting of vision and purpose! For others, however, especially those within the structure of a denomination, it was a definite and courageous step out of the box.

The atmosphere in the convention center where we met for that first 'Global Day' was charged to the brim. Any one of us could have stood at the podium and recited the alphabet and it would have been met with shouts of praise to God! We all knew we were onto something that came from and touched back at the very Heart of God.

This was no new concept to Jesus. From eternity past He had always moved and worked and created and expressed Himself in total *sumphoneo*. That's the Bible word for the dynamic agreement Jesus calls for in Matthew 18:19. It's how God does things. When He spoke of the work of Satan, the 'prince of this world', he said, "He has no hold on me … I do exactly what my Father has commanded me." [94] How could Satan possibly stand between the dynamic unity of Trinity agreement? [95]

Sumphoneo is obviously the route word for our 'symphony'. It isn't a string quartet; it's an elaborate musical composition involving many different parts. A symphony orchestra does not play after only a brief acquaintance or a superficial involvement; it takes practice, commitment discipline and time. Each member must not only hone his own skill, but must also learn to harmonize his gift with those of others. There's a submissiveness in symphony. In the same way, *sumphoneo* agreement doesn't come easily or quickly. But it can come when hearts are right, when leaders are servants and when men are friends, first.

And sumphoneo is costly! Even the practical step of leaving our 'places of worship' on a Sunday morning to gather as one church in one place took courage. It was a step of faith. For a start, we knew that some of our congregation would simply stay home! The simple element of

---

94   John 14:30,31
95   More about sumphoneo agreement in "Marked for Life" and "Choices" by Bill Davidson

going to a different place, with a different crowd, at a different time is enough to persuade some to think twice about leaving the comforts of home. The devil knows all too well that it doesn't take much to deter the army of God. A simple change of routine will probably do it for many of the soldiers!

On this point I can only express myself candidly. It *blows my mind* that anyone would stay home on such an occasion, but stay some did! Being pragmatists, we pastors were aware that not all our members tithe and some of those who do, do so infrequently, the pattern being that if they don't attend, they don't tithe. To give the benefit of the doubt I must assume that when they don't tithe, neither do they get paid! So we knew that we would 'take a hit' financially if we chose to take this step of meeting as one church. The outcome was that as well as meeting the expenses of the event, the 'hit' for many congregations was around one-thousand dollars. "Worth it at twice the price," I say!

Ask those who attended the Global Day of Prayer in 2007 what their high moment was and I am sure they would recall the signing of our pastors' covenant. This covenant was a statement of values and intent which mirrored the lifestyle we pastors had grown into over the years since making our decision to meet together. Our friendships had deepened to the point where we were no longer concerned about keeping up appearances. We had become real people and we were beginning to form some ideas about the real church. The barriers were falling not only between us, but also between our congregations. We had begun to ask the question, 'How many Churches,' even to the point of ceasing to call ourselves distinct and separate Churches and referring to ourselves as *congregations* within one Church. However, we understood that changing our vocabulary was a big step, but not enough. What was taking place was not a matter of terminology; it was a matter of covenant.

A Pastors' Covenant was composed on our behalf by Steve VanDixhorn, pastor of the Pine Knolls Alliance Church. Steven understood as well as any of us what it meant to walk in the depth of relationship to which God was calling us. His congregation had grown to several hundred; a 'first' for our region. He could well have walked on without the rest of us. As a member of the Christian Missionary Alliance, he and his congregation belonged to a mature and established denomination. It would have been easy for him to steer clear of those Pentecostals, Independents and Charismatics across town, but his integrity and his love for the Body of Christ dismissed any initial misgivings.

On Pentecost Sunday, 2007, the pastors of Adirondack Churches Together lined up to sign the covenant document. As profound and meaningful as the moment was, we were not accompanied by a solemn silence. The place sounded more as if we were lining up to receive our Olympic medals or – more to my liking – as if we'd just won the F.A. Cup in London's Wembley Stadium! That day, the Church roared like a mighty lion. Paul would have approved.

Life Group Discussion
Chapter 9: The Mosaic

A pastor of a great Church in Argentina once stated that he believed he could gauge the possibilities for genuine revival in a city by the level of unity among the pastors.

Questions for Discussion

1. From 1 to 10, what grade would you give the Churches in your city for their unity, cooperation and loving interaction in the Body of Christ?

2. What do you think you can do – as a group and as individuals – to make things better?

3. Are the congregations around you competitive or cooperative? How about You?

"It would be a grave sin to tell people there is no Hell below us and above us only sky, or even to imagine such a thing. But the greater sin would be to admit the existence of God, Hell and Heaven, but to delude people into thinking they are saved by some means other than that which God recognizes."

4. This danger is not just found in some orthodox churches where people might think that mere attendance at a ritual gets them into Heaven. Is it possible that people attend your congregation without ever seeing genuine conversion come about? Can mere attendance in your meetings give people the impression of being secure in God? What can you do to make sure this isn't the case?

10

The Covenant

We stood in line, surrounded by a wall of sound from that great mix of congregations. The crowd had no prior seating arrangements – "them over there, our Church here". It was beginning to feel like One People, One Church – at least for a day. Steve read the Covenant, for all to hear, then one by one we signed our names; not something God takes lightly.

Here is the Covenant of Adirondack Churches Together (ACT)

Father in heaven,

As pastors and leaders, we admit that the Body of Christ in the Greater Glens Falls region has presented a distorted picture of You.

- *While You are a God of unity, we have been divided.*
- *While You are generous to us, the undeserving, we have, through attitudes and actions, withheld the grace of friendship and care from those whose lives are broken.*
- *While You are the God of truth, we have chosen to walk in the shadows by giving preference to our image rather than to our true character.*

- *While You relentlessly pursue the lost, we have withdrawn from the most needy, choosing to focus most of our time, energy and resources on those who are already redeemed.*
- *While You are a great and good God, we have chosen to rely on our wisdom and strength rather than upon You.*
- *While You look upon the heart, we have chosen to focus on externals, denominational labels, styles of worship, and peripheral doctrinal issues.*

We repent of the pride, fear, self-sufficiency, competition, and dishonesty that have fractured Your beautiful Body. Before You and these witnesses, we covenant to:

- *Join together as co-laborers, rather than to view each other as competitors.*
- *Pray for one another, endeavoring to live out Christ's command to bear one another's burdens.*
- *Rejoice as other congregations experience God's blessing and to mourn when congregations experience division or loss.*
- *Guard our tongues lest we diminish the standing of a leader in the Body of Christ through careless words.*
- *Seek to open avenues for communication and, through communication, to live in unity, for when we stand in unity there we will experience Your commanded blessing.*
- *Celebrate our common standing as children of the living God through faith in Jesus Christ.*
- *Rejoice in our unique histories, personalities, and experiences, believing your design for the Church includes diversity.*
- *Make the goal of knowing, experiencing, and expressing Christ our highest aim, that He might receive honor and glory.*

As we signed that document, something happened. It was as if we were allowed to take a glimpse behind a long-drawn curtain to view what Church could be and should be. The challenge, however, is turning back from that view of the possible to deal with the probable and the present. Seeing things as they should be is seldom comfortable, especially when we are so aware of how things are. So, what is our reality?

Jean and I have the distinction of having been in ministry in this area since the late 1970s. We founded Church of The Nations in Lake Luzerne in 1981. The King's School was founded two years later and by God's grace they both still flourish today. So we have the ability to compare how things used to be in our region with how things now are.

When we first arrived in Upstate New York we were met with extraordinary kindness from the local people. Although we descended into a small rural village we found none of the insular small mindedness for which such communities are famous. I suppose we were something of a novelty, with our English accents and strange customs – a difference that still remains, however hard we try to 'go native' – but we experienced genuine friendship and acceptance.

Between the Churches, however, it was another matter; there was little warmth and almost no communication. In fact, all the maladies of inter-church competition - recruiting from one another's congregations, welcoming in the malcontents of another flock, open criticism of the Church down the road, even from the pulpit - these were all present and thriving. It was obvious that the prevailing spirits of independence and self-sufficiency had invaded the Church and too many members of congregations had never been delivered from them on their way into the kingdom!

One of the most destructive examples of this competitive spirit is gossip. Paul classifies gossip alongside "wickedness and depravity." [96] This wicked, divisive spirit was in evidence one evening as we sat with friends at dinner in their Queensbury home. They had invited us and a

---

96 Romans 1:29

recent convert who attended another congregation which was 'over the mountain' in the same area as our first American church plant.

The visitor asked the usual questions about our background and how we ended up in the Adirondacks. We told him of our beginnings, founding Church of The Nations in Lake Luzerne.

"Ah, yes." He replied. "My pastor told me that's the church where the pastor ran off with his secretary!"

"That would hardly be possible." I replied. "I am the founding pastor, and as for my secretary, she was the one who ran off, to the mission field!"

I followed up our little table-talk with a few choice comments. "There was indeed a pastor who chose to divorce his young wife and marry another woman in the Church. But that was another ministry which was in place before we came to the United States. It closed its doors and moved out of town. Soon after that we began our work and we bought the buildings belonging to that other ministry. But here's the sad thing," I continued, and I could see I had his attention. "Why would your pastor feel it necessary to pass on slanted information to you about something that happened twenty years ago, especially as you've only been a member of his congregation for less than a year?"

I knew why. He was making sure that an evening with the Davidsons didn't attract his new convert away from his flock! Call it what you will - fear, paranoia, competitive spirit, or just plain old fashioned rudeness - gossip causes division in the Body of Christ, and it was all too prevalent in our early years in our region. Add to that the climate of opposition to anything 'evangelical' or non-Catholic in the minds of much of the population and we had a hard row to plow.

Obviously that is why God gave Jean and me a verse to live by as we prepared to enter the Adirondack region. I asked for guidance as we began our new season of ministry. He led me to Psalm 37:

"Trust in the Lord and do good.
Dwell in the land and cultivate faithfulness." [97]

That's not much of a promise! The call to cultivate faithfulness is God's way of saying "You'll probably feel like quitting up ahead. Stay strong."

What our region needed was what it eventually got. Over the years of walking out our lives in Adirondack Churches Together we managed to approach that depth, that reality; that ground of trust that cannot abide the falsehood of an old competitive spirit. But you might ask where that covenant has taken us?

Several things have happened as a direct result. First of all, our region has been blessed! In fact I believe we edged into a glimpse of what we call 'The Commanded Blessing'. I take this from Psalm 133 which speaks of brothers dwelling together in unity. The last words are, "For there the Lord commanded the blessing." [98] It is one thing to be blessed but quite another to be under a blessing God has 'commanded' into place in response to the obedience of His followers living in unity agreement.

As a direct result – or so I believe – our region experienced a period of comparative prosperity in the midst of a world-wide financial recession. It was no Gold Rush. No oil wells were discovered. But the very fact that we did not slow down when other regions were collapsing was noteworthy. In the early 1900s Glens Falls was named 'The most progressive small city in the United States,' and whereas we are far from that now, a report appeared in U.S. News and World Report, ranking

---

97   Psalm 37:3 (New American Standard Version)
98   Psalm 133:3 (New King James Version)

Glens Falls as number two in the top ten housing markets for appreciation in the coming decade. The city was also ranked on a national basis
as one of the safest Downtown cities in which to live. Our 'main drag'
was ranked highly among places to do business in New York State!
Move over, Wall Street, here comes Glen Street!

But what of the Church - did the commanded blessing rush like a
mighty wind through the local congregations of worshipping people?
To answer that I make an interesting comparison, not this time with
the New Testament church, but with the early days of the Charismatic
Movement.

In the late 1960s and early 1970s a tremendous outpouring of the
Holy Spirit hit the traditional world of the denominations. Hundreds
of thousands of believers were affected, but one factor was fairly common. We would hear of groups of believers moving – some might say
they were being carried along despite themselves – into new ways of
worshipping and 'doing Church'. It was not always the case but we
often heard of their pastors and leaders lagging behind. This did little
to deter Church members who forged ahead, spending countless hours
in prayer and praise, organizing public meetings and even founding
thousands of new Churches. However, as the pastors of Adirondack
Churches Together have moved closer to Christ's ideal for His Church,
there has been a conspicuous difference with the days of the Charismatic
Renewal. The pastors seem to be ahead of the people! Not a bad place
for leaders to be, but only if the people follow!

Our Global Day of Prayer climaxed with the signing of the covenant.
After that momentous meeting there were shouts to "do this every
month". But even quarterly calls to worship and prayer have proved
a little too much for most people's busy schedules and the Global
Day events, although attracting hundreds of faithful attendees, have
diminished in size as the years have progressed. Also, the event has
been moved from the Sunday morning slot it so powerfully occupied

– which caused greater sacrifice for the more traditional among us with congregations giving up their time-honored traditions – and it now takes place on a benign Sunday evening; often seen as "of secondary importance" to the Sunday morning meeting by most congregations and a time when the priority is getting ready for the busy week ahead!

This leads us to yet another comparison with our relatives back in New Testament days and even those of the 60s and 70s. It is evident that they lived in a world far less busy than ours, or so we assume! Busy-ness has invaded our Western culture to a ridiculous degree. I am reminded of the Disney song, "Busy doing nothing, working the whole day through, trying to find lots of things not to do." I dispute that we are, in fact, busier than simpler days in simpler societies. I have regularly visited areas where the women wake at 4:00am to begin making the first (and often 'only') meal of the day – all from scratch. And yet we zap our toasted breakfast strudel in the microwave and dash out the door. We are too busy to make anything else. Our lives are under constant bombardment by the demands of our digital appendages which – at the sound of the downloaded anthems of our choice – provoke us to spring to attention like footmen and maids responding to the bells in the servant's quarters of some grand Victorian Manor House, to do the bidding of our masters.

The women in our community, who once gave time and energy to raising great kids and providing a safe, happy and well nourished home environment, now give up on much of that because of the sheer necessity – or so we have told ourselves – of a second income. After all, we have to get the kids through college and pay their way until - somewhere around the age of twenty-seven - they might begin to support themselves! For the Mom who dares to stay home, she is but a taxi driver to the busy schedule of the children – and several of their friends. Again, they just have to get on the team because how else are they going to get a scholarship for college? Some families will even move house and home and abandon the covenant membership of their local Church, just so their kids can get on a better school team and be noticed by the scouts. And on that day when they hear the Lord of the Universe tell them "I never knew you," [99] their kids can reply, "Well, at least I played linebacker for Syracuse!"

I once told a dear friend from Japan how difficult it is in the U.S. to organize anything in the Church for teens, considering the demands on families ferrying their kids, often to more than one extra-curricular event in the same night. She replied, "It's the same in Japan. One night it's Math Club, another night, Science Team, then it's off to English Language class and later that night, Mandarin Chinese." Whoops! I just meant that American Moms were stressed out getting one kid to hockey and the other to soccer!

So, as we pastors grow closer, considering the idea of "one Church in the city," I don't always see evidence of willingness in the congregations to grow any closer than they are right now; and that only involves occasional meetings.

How strange. I come from a generation that saw revolution on the streets, changing entire societies, and I now watch the present-day Islamic world being reshaped by brave protesters. But in all of this I wonder what it will take to awaken the Church to revolutionary action. Present day Christians work on the Lord's Day because the boss would fire them otherwise. They remain mute when told they are not allowed to pray or worship in public areas even vaguely connected to the State. They watch as fellow-workers who are Muslim get allocated prayer rooms and time off to pray during the day, but they "can't make it to Church" once a week because of the pressure of work. Presumably, in order to desire change, one has to be discontent with the status quo and free from a position of laissez-faire.

I believe the Church may well be ripe for such a shaking and as in Bible times God has many secular agents in powerful places who will willingly

---

99   Matthew 7:23

provide His people with the required shock to their dormant system. For instance, let's consider how well we do in the stewardship of our property. Is this an area in which we might soon be shaken towards unity and away from our complacent individualism? It should be! Each congregation in our town either owns or, leases a set of buildings in which to do their Church business. In 1995 we founded Church of The King in Queensbury and only a few years later built our fine ministry center for a few hundred thousand dollars. Our mortgage is low – we owe the bank around $300,000.00. But because of the development around us our property is assessed at well over $1,000.000.00. This major asset will continue to appreciate in the years to come, especially as the State University of New York across the road adds its new dorm facilities and dozens of condos and town houses are erected right next door.

Since we founded our church a few new ministries have been established and have set up shop within a mile of our location. (Gone are the days when people commuted forty miles to attend our meetings in Lake Luzerne!) Under strong leadership these congregations have grown to the point of purchasing their own facilities. So, here we sit, as separate, diverse aspects of the one Body of Christ, owning property within a mile of each other, valued at several million dollars and using these properties for a few hours each week. But what is that when compared to the church attended by some friends of ours in a Mid-Western State which recently put on an addition costing $30million!

Now consider what might happen if local authorities, under the squeeze from State and Federal cuts, begins to lean toward exacting property taxes from Not for Profit entities such as Churches. This one line-item alone would close most, if not every Church building in town, or at least fundamentally alter their budgets! Don't think that this is indefensible. I believe I received this little idea from God and I shared it with several groups of pastors, only to hear some weeks later that already, two New England States have approached Not for Profit corporations under their jurisdiction with the very same idea!

What would happen if this comes to your town? Would there be a sudden rush to unity as ministries found common cause to believe in unified collective stewardship of property, thinking up ways for several ministries to use the same facility. It's easy, really… Just consider the idea of ministry teams made up of apostles, prophets, evangelists, pastors and teachers, working together to care for the entire flock of believers under their care – using a shared facility in whatever way the Lord leads them; somewhat like First Church of Jerusalem.

The Early Church was described in this way: "On the day called the Day of the Sun [100] all who live in cities or in the country gather together to one place, and the memoirs of the apostles or the writings of the prophets are read, as long as time permits; then, when the reader has ceased, the president verbally instructs and exhorts to the imitation of these things." [101] Did you notice, "all" the believers gathered together in one place. Imagine the power, the synergy, the sumphoneo! But why wait until some local government shakes us into unifying action. Why not do it for the sake of the unity of Christ's Body! Everyone who has attended our (for want of a much better word) "inter-church" meetings senses the incredible dynamic that rises up in the worship, the sheer joy of being together. So imagine the influence of a powerfully unified congregation meeting in the center of the region, rather than dozens of the best-kept secrets in town meeting in their little clubhouses. What a different dynamic in that unified congregation than in the crowd of the mega Church! Could it be possible that the Head of The Church is just waiting to pour out something even more dynamic in response: a Commanded Blessing? So what's holding us back? I suppose the answer is simple. We are still many Churches and not One.

O, The Methodists they want to join us, A move that we would not condemn,
So long as they're uniting with us, And we're not uniting with them! [102]

---

100 Sunday; the first day of the working week.
101 Justin Martyr: The First Apology (155 AD) Chapter 67 'Weekly Worship of the Christians'.
102 From "The Church Is" – a comedy by Bill Davidson

Life Group Discussion
Chapter 10: The Covenant

Let's begin by reading the Covenant featured in this chapter. It would be good if we all participate and take one section each, around the group.

Questions for Discussion

1. What section of The Covenant impresses you most as being vital to unity in a region of the Body of Christ? What sections do you think might be the most difficult to keep?

2. What evidences are there in your region of definite moves toward Christ's Body coming into sumphoneo agreement? What can you do to prosper these, or create new ones?

3. What do you think the advantages/disadvantages would be for "all believers gathering together in one place?" Does this necessarily cause or help the unity of the Body?

In this chapter, Bill spoke of the predicament in which the Church would be if we did not enjoy the privilege of a non-taxable status, especially with property taxes. He wrote: "Now consider what might happen if local authorities, under the squeeze from State and Federal cuts, begin to lean toward exacting property taxes from Not for Profit entities such as churches. .... What would happen if this comes to your town?"

4. Well, what would happen?

5. Bill speaks of "the prevailing spirit" of The Adirondacks as being 'independence and self-sufficiency'. What is the prevailing spirit in your region? How has it manifested itself throughout history? If it is negative, what can you do to change it?

11

Some Assembly Required

Although it was significant, our Pastors' Covenant was merely a first step toward putting practical unity in place. The gap between our ideals and our reality would be our challenge. Our heart for genuine unity was evident but it was like those items we purchase that come with a handy manual, declaring, "Some assembly required." That usually means hours of frustration ahead, especially when the manual seems to have been composed by someone who has never attempted the job at hand and also has a distinct dislike for the English language. Our manual proved to be a blend of the simplicity of Scripture, the complexity of Church History and large chunks of cultural pluralistic individualism and self-determinism. A difficult blend!

We knew it would be risky to put our names to a covenant document. We had a feeling God would expect us to live up to it and make it real. The question before us was simple: were we willing to lay our lives down to see the resurrection of the Church of Jesus Christ in all her glory? Were we willing to allow God to put the pieces back together?

Scripture speaks of the Church this way:

"Let us rejoice and be glad and give him glory!
For the wedding of the Lamb has come,
and his bride has made herself ready . [103]

And that bride has a certain appearance about her.

"That he might present it to himself a glorious church,
not having spot, or wrinkle, or any such thing;
but that it should be holy and without blemish. [104]

In my experience, spots are a sign of immaturity, and wrinkles a sign of old age and ill health. Neither belongs to the Church! There should be a few 'laugh lines,' but that's all!

Our Pastors' Covenant is the stuff that mature Church is made of. It demands action and choices which are rare where Church is concerned, but absolutely essential. I believe our Covenant is framed in a way of which Paul would approve. He spoke strongly to the Churches of his generation: "I urge you, brothers, to watch out for those who cause divisions and put obstacles in your way." [105] And, "I appeal to you, brothers, in the name of our Lord Jesus Christ, that all of you agree with one another so that there may be no divisions among you and that you may be perfectly united in mind and thought." [106] I have to laugh, imagining the faces of the congregation as one of the Corinthian elders first read this next bit: "I have no praise for you, for your meetings do more harm than good. In the first place, I hear that when you come together as a Church, there are divisions among you, and to some extent I believe it." [107]

Happily, we all know that Paul is not about to walk in on our congregations. He has no facility to bring judgment on us save that which he

103 Revelation 19:7
104 Ephesians 5:27 (King James Version)
105 Romans 16:17
106 1 Corinthians 1:10-11
107 1 Corinthians 11:17-19

has already written, and that is judgment enough! But we should at least consider the significance of the fact that the Holy Spirit is already in the midst of our congregations! So, free from the burden of offending Paul, let's assess where we might be offending the Spirit. Let's take a look at some of the meat of that covenant, asking ourselves, "Are we guilty of offending you, Lord, or are we living in ways that befit The Bride?"

Here are the 'line items' of our covenant commitment to change – our covenant response:

1. *As pastors and leaders, we admit that the Body of Christ in the Greater Glens Falls region has presented a distorted picture of You.*

There are two serious crimes, attempted by those who try to hide their culpability for wrong doing; "withholding evidence" and "tampering with evidence." Withholding evidence is an obstruction of justice caused by stifling or suppression of evidence with the knowledge that it is being sought. Tampering with evidence is the crime of altering, destroying, or concealing physical evidence with the intent to affect the outcome of a criminal investigation or court proceeding. Both are a serious crime, usually a felony, which means that a conviction can result in years in prison and a large fine.

A silent Church is guilty on both counts. A Church which appears to care little for the lost and speaks seldom of their redemption is withholding evidence. Members, who treat their Christian brothers and sisters with contempt by becoming easily offended, separating, splitting and dividing, present a distorted picture of Christ's Body. They are tampering with the evidence of the resurrection and apostleship of Christ.[108]

The entire Bible is a testimony to one great truth; the Character of

---

108 John 17:21 (The term 'apostle' means 'a sent one')

God. When we display character traits that are less than loving and full of self we do a disservice to His Character. "His intent was that now, *through the Church*, the manifold wisdom of God should be made known." [109] "For God, who said, 'Let light shine out of darkness,' made his light shine in our hearts to give us the light of the knowledge of the glory of God in the face of Christ." [110] What a challenge to think that the world will see Christ in His mirror, the Church. "We, who with unveiled faces all reflect the Lord's glory." [111]

> 2. *While You are the God of truth, we have chosen to walk in the shadows by giving preference to our image rather than to our true character.*

Actually, that which we choose to show to the world *is* our true character. This statement refers to that which we *should* show; what Christ desires to show through us. Any adjustment we make to the Body of Christ, attempting to make her image more attractive to a blinded world is a needless distortion. Jesus said, "Go out into the highways and hedges, and compel them to come in, that my house may be filled." [112] Any compelling we do will rightly be seen as coercion and manipulation. However, there is a beauty in Jesus which is compelling enough, even to the most degraded of humans; in fact *especially* compelling to the most degraded. Only to the eyes of the self righteous and religious has He become common-place. Our place is to allow His compelling beauty to show through our Church life, and not to go on trusting in our abilities, our preacher's gifts or our excellent music to appear attractive to a blinded and deaf world?

> 3. *While You relentlessly pursue the lost, we have withdrawn from the most needy, choosing to focus most of our time, energy and resources on those who are already redeemed.*

---

109 Ephesians 3:10
110 2 Corinthians 4:6
111 2 Corinthians 3:18
112 Luke 14:23 (King James Version)

C. S. Lewis wrote, "We are shy nowadays of even mentioning heaven. We are afraid of the jeer about 'pie in the sky'." [113] That might have been Lewis's dilemma in the mid 20th Century, but this following century is filled with people who assume Heaven but deny the other place. Do Christians believe in Hell? If we did, we would be wracked with concern over the plight of the lost. *Sinners in the Hands of an Angry God* [114] is a figment of our history. No longer can we hope to dangle our hearers over the flames of Hell. Why would we even try? Our hearers are probably all saved in any case. And the world is immune to such talk, numbed by nightly slices of horror, murder, vampirism, immorality and massacre. Who could hope to shock them by means of the threat of Hades? The profound tragedy of school massacres may not be as senseless as it first appears. It may simply be the outcome of a shout – a scream of rage – at a world which has become inured to anything less than the hideous.

We may rush to claim doctrinal purity when some author claims Hell no longer exists, but do we live as if it does. Hell hath no fury in the heart of a complacent Church. And if there is a Hell, it doesn't say much for our home town when Christians tell their friends that their lost loved ones have "Gone to a better place!" A modern author might sell more books by saying, "How could a God of love send sinners to a horrible Hell. Isn't He a God of love?" But the Author of all things has clearly stated that there is a Hell – a place of separation from Him and all He is, His sustaining grace, His amazing mercy, His protecting love. True, God will never send anyone to Hell, but He will, broken-heartedly, allow them to go where they'll receive exactly what they've always asked for – separation from Him. "The wicked shall be turned into hell, and all the nations that forget God." [115] God knows there is a Hell, but the Silent Church isn't telling.

4. *While You are a great and good God, we have chosen to rely on our wisdom and strength rather than upon You.*

---

113 C.S.Lewis – 'The Problem of Pain'
114 Jonathan Edwards (1703 – 1758) preached this sermon in Enfield, Connecticut on July 8, 1741.
115 Psalm 9:17 (New King James Version)

We don't tell people about Hell for one good reason; they might not find the message to their liking, and then how would we attract them to ourselves or to our only strategy, our meetings?

We have all heard the phrase, "Well, there's good news and there's bad news. Which do you want first?" However, a tendency in the modern Church is to present the message of the good news while pretending there is no bad; misrepresenting the fact that the consequences of refusing the good are bad; really bad!

The One who knows best how to communicate the gospel is constantly nudging at every elbow and knocking on every heart's door. The Holy Spirit has rightly been called 'The Divine Evangelist' and 'The Hound of Heaven.' I like that last one because once a hound gets a scent he is totally focused on his prey. In that tiny representation of His creation God shows something of His character; He relentlessly pursues the lost. But He makes it abundantly clear as He lovingly pursues, that there is an "If not" to every call and promise. He says, "But if you do not do what is right, sin is crouching at your door; it desires to have you, but you must master it." [116] And, "But if you do not drive out the inhabitants of the land, those you allow to remain will become barbs in your eyes and thorns in your sides. They will give you trouble." [117] He makes it clear, "If you do not carefully follow all the words of this law, which are written in this book, and do not revere this glorious and awesome name — the Lord your God — the Lord will send fearful plagues on you and your descendants, harsh and prolonged disasters, and severe and lingering illnesses," [118] and "if you do not obey the Lord, and if you rebel against his commands, his hand will be against you." [119]

God is not shy about letting people know of the consequences of their disobedience. He would be unloving if He chose not to. His

116 Genesis 4:7
117 Numbers 33:55
118 Deuteronomy 28:58,59
119 1 Samuel 12:15

law shows up our wrongness, but law without consequence is merely good advice.

5. *While You look upon the heart, we have chosen to focus on externals, denominational labels, styles of worship, and peripheral doctrinal issues.*

Let's face it, the denominations might have come about because of doctrinal differences, but many Christians are not doctrinally linked to their church, it's a simple case of preference. We like the style, the atmosphere, the convenience of the "Church of our choice". We are, after all, consumers in a consumer society. We pay for what we prefer and shop elsewhere when our preferences are not served.

The first part of the covenant concluded with a repentant recognition of our sin. *"We repent of the pride, fear, self-sufficiency, competition, and dishonesty that have fractured Your beautiful Body."* It continued with a response, a commitment to action. True repentance is a choice to stop a certain behavior, turn around, and choose differently. As a response, God's grace rushes in to empower us in the endeavor. The next steps of the covenant take us from repentance to responsive action:

We covenant to join together as co-laborers, rather than to view each other as competitors. We will pray for one another, endeavoring to live out Christ's command to bear one another's burdens and rejoice as other congregations experience God's blessing and to mourn when congregations experience division or loss.

We will guard our tongues lest we diminish the standing of a leader in the Body of Christ through careless words and seek to open avenues for communication so that we may live in unity, for when we stand in unity there we will experience Your commanded blessing. We commit to celebrate our common standing as children of the living God through faith in Jesus Christ and rejoice in our unique histories, personalities, and experiences, believing that Your design for the Church includes diversity.

We make the goal of knowing, experiencing, and expressing Christ our highest aim, that He might receive honor and glory!

The signing of this covenant brought the pastors of Adirondack Churches Together to a watershed moment. I believe it pleased God that we came that far but how to please Him from that point onward was quite another thing. Being 'one in the Spirit' sounded good - who could disagree with that, in principle? But how 'one' could we become? And we were the pastors, the leaders, but what about those we were supposed to be leading? Our congregations were occupied by hundreds of people who had been trained to live in a pluralistic society based on personal choice and rugged individualism. Would they respond to a call to submit their precious free market preferences for the sake of sumphoneo?

A place to begin would be to try to stop the migration of members – I call them "Charismatic Butterflies" - from flitting from congregation to congregation at a whim or, more often than not, as a response to an offense, real or perceived. Such behavior is a certain way to cause divisions between congregations. In the past, God has used the transfer of members from one part of the Body of Christ to another to strengthen the gene-pool. The Reformation is all about that. William Booth would not have seen the thousands flocking into the kingdom had he remained in The Wesleyan New Connection. These were bold steps taken by people who heard from God. The "Butterflies," however, are transfers of a different species, usually creating chasms where bridges would be best.

For generations one of the most ignored passages of scripture is this exhortation from Jesus Himself, "If another believer sins against you, go privately and point out the fault. If the other person listens and confesses it, you have won that person back. But if you are unsuccessful, take one or two others with you and go back again, so that everything you say may be confirmed by two or three witnesses. If that person still refuses to listen, take your case to the Church. If the Church decides you are right, but the other person won't accept it, treat that person as a pagan or a corrupt tax collector." [120]

The first instruction is to "go to your brother," not to your friends or even to your intercessory group where you can 'share a concern'. That's gossip! And neither does Jesus say you should go tell your pastor so that he can deal with it. No, that turns him into a hireling… Isn't that what we pay our hired-help for, to do the work we'd rather not do ourselves?

I've lost count of people who have left our congregation out of what they claimed was an offense. But the actual reason they left was that they simply refused to obey the command of Jesus Christ and deal with the offense. Seldom do these wandering souls realize the wounds they leave behind and they certainly don't consider the cancer they are carrying into their new spiritual body. We pastors tried to stop the rot, but short of pulling up the drawbridge it has proved almost impossible to prevent some consumers from switching supermarkets at the slightest offense.

Continuing our comparison with the Early Church we conclude that it was a great deal easier for Paul when he commanded discipline of a member of the Corinthian congregation. [121] For that person, there was nowhere else to go. These days a member under discipline can simply "pop in down the road" and even receive a warm welcome. In medieval times, the mere threat of excommunication was enough to bring kings to their knees. Nowadays, however, there is too often a welcoming embrace from one congregation as a rebel tears his (or her) limb from the body of another. In our area one entire worship band left

120 Matthew 18:15-17 (New Living Translation)
121 1 Corinthians, Chapter 5

a congregation in disappointment and disarray only to be leading in worship in another in a matter of days. Everyone loves Church growth but the idea of growth through conversion, rather than through transfer, would be a novel concept. Has the number of believers actually increased in any city where a Mega Church has appeared?

Life Group Discussion
Chapter 11: Some Assembly Required

It is doubtful that your group will finish this session in one sitting.
It may take several!
But it will be worthwhile not to miss one line of it!

The Pastors' Covenant contained these six powerful statements. Let's begin by reading them, taking one statement each around our group.

1. *As pastors and leaders, we admit that the Body of Christ in the Greater Glens Falls region has presented a distorted picture of You.*
2. *While You are a God of unity, we have been divided. While You are generous to us, the undeserving, we have, through attitudes and actions, withheld the grace of friendship and care from those whose lives are broken.*
3. *While You are the God of truth, we have chosen to walk in the shadows by giving preference to our image rather than to our true character.*
4. *While You relentlessly pursue the lost, we have withdrawn from the most needy, choosing to focus most of our time, energy and resources on those who are already redeemed.*
5. *While You are a great and good God, we have chosen to rely on our wisdom and strength rather than upon You.*
6. *While You look upon the heart, we have chosen to focus on externals, denominational labels, styles of worship, and peripheral doctrinal issues.*

Questions for Discussion

a. Are there any statements above to which you relate?
b. These statements are to be taken as a whole, but – for the sake of discussion - which one do you think is the worst condition; the most costly?

c. In the light of 2 Chronicles 7:14, what is God's promised response to this sort of confession?

Bill writes that he believes Matthew 18:15-17 has been *"one of the most ignored passages of scripture"*. Read through those verses again (from the text shown in the chapter) and list below the steps which Jesus taught us to take at times of offense.

4. If another believer sins against you, what do you do first?
5. If you are unsuccessful, who do you take with you, and why?
6. If that person still refuses to listen, what is your next option?

God can use the 'cross-pollination' of believers moving from one part of the Body of Christ to another, but there are many times when transfers are born out of unresolved conflicts. If you hear of something of this nature, what should you do?

a. Call the pastor and ask what happened
b. Call the pastor and ask him to follow it up
c. Find out what the offense was all about then share it with your prayer partners
d. Pray about it and leave it to those who are directly involved
e. Write an anonymous letter to the offended party
f. Stay out of it and hope that 'all things work together for the good'

And if it's 'none of the above' then what is your strategy?

12

What Shape, the Church?

It looked more like a skateboard than the chassis of an automobile, and that's exactly what General Motors called it – the Skateboard. It was the outcome of GM's innovative idea of calling several young engineers together to form a think-tank on the future of the car. No suggestions were dismissed. Brain-storming was the order of the day. Creativity exploded with every new idea.

"Why do we have to all face the front? Can't we sit in a circle so we can talk?"

"Does the diver always have to sit up front?"

"If the engine is electrical and computerized, why can't we just change it by downloading a new one?" The "car" would never be the same!

Now, if the Church was a fresh idea, birthed out of the first half of the 21st Century, what shape would it take? Just like the GM Skateboard was only workable in the real world if that slim chassis held all the components necessary to drive the car, so the Church would only be viable if attached to the foundations already prescribed by the Builder. Paul describes them... "For no one can lay any foundation other than the one already laid, which is Jesus Christ." [122] And, "God's household, built on the foundation of the apostles and prophets, with Christ Jesus himself as the chief cornerstone." [123]

Once we have the foundational rock of Jesus in place and apostolic and prophetic ministries prayerfully leading and equipping all the body-parts to do the work of service, the rest depends on the vision and imagination of the congregation and its leaders to be free and flexible enough to follow the leading of the Holy Spirit. [124]

It's exciting to think up what the shape of the Church would be if she had just been born. Would we buy buildings in which to hold meetings or would we meet in each other's homes, using large public venues for our Celebrations? Would all the believers meet together or would we separate into factions? How often would we meet? Would meetings be the main events of Church life, as they seem to be today, or would other expressions take precedence? How would we tell people about the good news of Jesus Christ? Would we make it our natural business to tell it to the world and take it to the streets, or would we hope that the lost would somehow get it through osmosis? Come on… think about it! Because if we answer that we would do things differently, then one question remains: Why don't we?

I was brought up in a rather conservative evangelical tradition. However, upon entering the William Booth ministry training college in London I was chosen to be part of the very first guitar twanging contemporary Christian group. At first it was a simple "photo-shoot", but within days we were playing new songs on national television. A few weeks later we were firmly in the Pop Charts sitting alongside The Beatles, and several other lads from Liverpool, my home town. [125]

---

122 1 Corinthians 3:10, 11
123 Ephesians 2:19,20
124 Ephesians 4:11-16
125 More of the story of The Joystrings can be found in "Marked for Life" and "Choices" by Bill Davidson

For the next few years my fellow Joystrings and I were propelled out of our denominational box and into the world. Tuesdays were spent driving out of London to some location north of the city. Two days of camera rehearsals followed. By Thursday night we'd be ready to record our half-hour national TV Show, filled with contemporary Christian songs we'd just composed. And why did we compose our own material? Simply because there was no such thing as Contemporary Christian Music before we came on the scene!

Our programs were broadcast every Sunday evening. By that time, however, we would be in some auditorium elsewhere in the UK, or Sweden, Norway, The Netherlands – you name it, we were there. We spent more time singing and talking to the non-Christian members of society than we did with fellow Christians in Church services. When we did appear in Church it was not unknown for the Vicar [126] to reconsecrate his altar before Sunday Matins, upon hearing of our unconventional visit to his palace of Gothic splendor the night before, which - by the way - had been packed with rowdy sinners, crowding in to hear about Jesus! No wonder he felt the need to 'cleanse' the place.

In the mid1960s there was a period of fourteen months when I did not attend a 'traditional' Church service. Then, one Sunday morning, I found myself back home in London, so I slipped in to one of the best Churches in our denomination. As I sat there, familiar as I was to taking the gospel to the world in some of the most 'worldly' of places, I suffered what can only be called 'culture-shock.' I could no more relate to what was being said and sung than if I'd walked in on a group of strangers. And yet this was the Church of my childhood, the Church of my theological and ministry training, the Church of my ordination.

I had been given the immeasurable privilege of experiencing the Church in all her splendor. Church in concert halls, Church in Liverpool's 'Cavern Club', Church in theaters, Church in night clubs, Church in

126 An Anglican Priest

town halls, Church in stadiums, Church in EMI's Abbey Road studios and even Church for three nights-running in London's Playboy Club. And you've never had Church until the Playboy Bunnies have broken their own rules and danced to the music!

It was precisely because of that last engagement that our tour of the United States was cancelled for the summer of 1968. Taking the gospel to the Playboy community – even although it was, in reality, a few dozen tired businessmen sitting having dinner, served by waitresses in ridiculously tight satin swimsuits with outrageous pink ears protruding from their bouffant 60s hairstyles – was too much for the conservatives across the Atlantic to appreciate – at least not publicly! So our tour was cancelled.

And yet I wonder where Jesus would have been that night; the same Jesus who gained the reputation of being a "glutton and a drunkard, and a friend of the worst sort of sinners!" [127] One thing with which I consol myself is that Jesus would probably not have been allowed to tour America's Bible Belt either, after it was revealed that "Levi invited Jesus and his disciples to be his dinner guests, along with his fellow tax collectors and many other notorious sinners. (There were many people of this kind among the crowds that followed Jesus.) But when some of the teachers of religious law saw him eating with people like that, they said to his disciples, "Why does he eat with such scum?" [128] Jesus' answer to the hypocrites of His generation is a clarion call to the Church: "Healthy people don't need a doctor — sick people do. I have come to call sinners, not those who think they are already good enough." [129] Of course, what Jesus really meant was, "There are none more sick than those who are dying from self-righteousness!"

There is only one reason for the Church to be upon this planet; that is to communicate the good news of Christ's redemptive death and

---

127 Matthew 11:19 (New Living Translation)
128 Mark 2:15,16
129 Mark 2:17

resurrection to a lost and dying world. God knows, everything else about Church would be better served in Heaven. However, He has left us here, and for one purpose alone; that we might "speed the day" of His return by taking the gospel to the world. Just as Peter said, "You ought to live holy and godly lives as you look forward to the day of God and speed its coming." [130] And I know of no other way to speed the coming of the Lord than to obey His command when He said, "this gospel of the kingdom will be preached in the whole world as a testimony to all nations, and then the end will come." [131]

What shape the Church that will accomplish this? Must it be shaped the same as the Church that has delayed His coming for two thousand years? Is it the Church that meets as "the best kept secret in town?" Perhaps it's the Church that does 99% of its business behind closed doors. Will the Silent Church accomplish the task?

It's time for a major reformation. No, I didn't say revival. A genuine one of those wouldn't be a bad idea, but the recent outpourings of the Holy Spirit – if they be real at all – have left many of us even more forgetful of the lost and only hungry for even more exciting meetings; as if the Spirit's outpoured splendor was for our own entertainment.

Let's consider some of the things we do; things with which we associate the Church. Take 'Communion' for instance. I love taking Communion with our Church family. After saying a few words and reading from the Scriptures I usually get to watch from the pulpit as my brothers and sisters in the Lord line up down the aisles to receive a little piece of bread and Welch's Grape Juice in a tiny plastic cup. I sense the deep significance of these moments and even in the midst of this most contemporary congregation which just "rocked out" to a powerful worship band, we partake of a long tradition dating way back through the history of the Church. Occasionally, however, I wonder to

---

130   2 Peter 3:12
131   Matthew 24:14

myself, "Did we ever have a Reformation?" And lovingly I chide my Church family (much of which has been converted from an Irish or Italian Catholic background) - and I include myself - at how 'Catholic' we still are!

Compare what we do, and how we do it, to the Lord's Table in the New Testament. Paul was disturbed to hear about how people were behaving in the Church in Corinth. "When you come together, it is not the Lord's Supper you eat, for as you eat, each of you goes ahead without waiting for anybody else. One remains hungry, another gets drunk. Don't you have homes to eat and drink in? Or do you despise the church of God and humiliate those who have nothing? What shall I say to you? Shall I praise you for this? Certainly not!" [132]

Can you imagine any of our generation getting drunk or being gluttonous over a morsel of bread or a thimble of fruit juice? It would seem that their 'Communion' – the Lord's Supper – was drastically different from that of which we partake. The original communion feast which Paul referred to - which we have sublimated into its essential elements - caused the Early Church to come under intense persecution. They called their celebration of the Lord's Supper 'The Love Feast' [133] and rumors of its elements soon spilled out to the pagan world outside. First of all, it was for "Members Only" and it was rumored that it consisted of a feast of love ending in "cannibalism and drinking blood!" No wonder word got around!

The reality is that 'feasting' is very much a part of the culture of the kingdom of God on earth, just as it seems to be in Heaven. It was certainly incorporated by God into the Hebrew life-style and it still exists in most Mediterranean cultures to this day. When Jesus "took the cup" [134] during The Last Supper, it was the Cup of Thanksgiving [135] which

---

132 1 Corinthians 11:20-22
133 Or 'The Agape Feast'
134 Matthew 26:27
135 Sometimes called 'The Cup of Salvation' or the 'Cup of Redemption' –   Psalm 116:13

was one of several cups of the Passover Feast. When Jesus speaks about entering the heart of a willing believer, He says, "Here I am! I stand at the door and knock. If anyone hears my voice and opens the door, I will come in and eat with him, and he with me." [136] The original word for "eat" was "dine" – meaning the principle meal of the day. No light snack; dinner! And upon entering into our eternal reward we will be invited to sit down at "the wedding supper of the Lamb!" [137] Again, the 'supper' in question is a full feast. The original word meant, 'dinner'. I wonder how many courses! The Early Church was known to meet regularly at each other's tables to 'break bread' together; more feasting! The historian and recorder, Pliny, when writing to the Emperor Trajan, wrote, "the Christians, after having met on a stated day in the early morning to address a form of prayer to Christ, as to a divinity, later in the day would reassemble to eat a common and harmless meal." [138]

There's something special about gathering around a table stacked with good food. God invented it – as it is in Heaven, so shall it be on earth! The Early Church appreciated the significance of that tradition. They knew it was more than feeding the face or fueling up. Not for them a hurried note from Mom, saying, "Dinner in the fridge." Only a few families in the modern Church ever sit to enjoy "breaking bread to-gether." Nowadays manufacturers of refrigerators boast an "easy-access drawer" at a child's eye level. When there's no-one else home, how else can a seven year-old serve himself dinner?

Every so often, our congregation in Church of The King celebrates Communion in the original way. The seats are moved to one side and our entire auditorium becomes a fine banquet hall. And this is not some weeknight event; it's Sunday Morning. It's that week's "Celebration" – worship, fellowship, the Word, and food. Just like in the New Testament Church – just like in Heaven.

---

136 Revelation 3:20
137 Revelation 19:9
138 Pliny to Trajan, Book 10, Letter 97

Although their purpose is to be more intimate than a public gathering, cell groups (we call them Life Groups) in the Church have an amazing way of becoming mini-meetings run by mini-pastors; an opening time of worship is followed by some announcements, a time of teaching from the Word and personal ministry. It's the only shape of Church most believers are used to. It's a wonder they don't take up an offering! Nothing wrong with that, you say; and you're right. But will someone get biblical and break out the food! Hearts and minds have a tendency to open up when mouths do the same.

I believe the shape of the Church should be as flexible and multi-faceted as that of the New Testament. From the beginning in Jerusalem, they enjoyed their times of worship and teaching standing alongside thousands of fellow believers. The Church also fitted in to everyday life with a dynamic that saw many more thousands attracted to their lifestyle. They were never squeezed into the world's mould, [139] and neither should we be. The Church is the body of an infinite God. Its shape is not defined by what we have been or by the preferences of one generation or another. We are shaped by one Hand. "Like clay in the hand of the potter," says God, "so are you in my hand." [140]

Do we need more flexibility? Consider how your world might change in the coming years? I often say, democracy means 'those with the most kids wins, in one generation.' By that I predict that Islam will take over Europe and invade the rest of the Western World without the necessity of a 'hot war'. Simple demographics will do it. They have the most children, compared with the average American family, which has 2.59 (God bless the 0.59!) So – again – will your world change? If so, what shape, your Church, in that changed environment?

We have already considered what might happen if cash-strapped states discontinue the practice of granting generous tax relief to Churches.

---

139 Romans 12:2 - J.B. Philips Translation
140 Jeremiah 18:6

Will it be seen as the 'civic duty' of ministries to share the load? How will that affect your Church's budget? I have often stirred the pot by challenging the complacent Christian attitude which defiantly says, "I don't trust the government with my health care!" and yet blithely entrusts children to state-run government schools which are under strict Federal mandates, one of which is the enforced absence of Christianity either from conversation or curriculum! Does this mean that the education of our children is less important than the condition of our health? What if Christians acted with integrity, not only making a noise about abortion and mandated health care, but also questioning the idea of the 'taxation without representation' of tax-funded schools which openly teach anti-Christian philosophy and refuse even the mention of That Name!

Since the 1980s the Church in America has learned a bit about protesting the ills of society but our rallies pale by comparison to the actions of the Early Church. Whereas the modern American Church might oppose the imposition of taxes on Christians to cater for a government mandated health care system, the first Christians actually *provided* the care that sick folk needed. The Early Church saw the needy as their responsibility. The love of Christ was so full in their hearts that they tended to overflow, and the world was changed by the residual effect! Do you recall what the Emperor Julian said in his complaint against the Christians? "The godless Galileans (*Christians*) care not only for their own poor but for ours as well; while those who belong to us look in vain for help."

Past generations of Christians invented hospitals, orphanages, and burial grounds. The Salvation Army invented the concept of the modern Travel Agency. How else would they be able to cope with the thousands being sent around the world with the gospel? The Army also created the first Employment Agency. The scum of the earth – those with whom Jesus spent most of His time – needed a job after they were radically converted!

We would see a revolutionary change in the shape and state of the modern Church if every time we are offended by the latest piece of legislation, instead of spitting our protest into the winds of change, we prayerfully consider what our alternative solution might be. People who think that way provoke their contemporaries to say, "These who have turned the world upside down have come here too." [141]

But how could we cope with the world's problems? Where would the money come from? Should we even be concerned with this world which one day soon will be burned up to make way for the coming age? [142] Well, it has been said, "If the Church in America would only tithe, we could feed the world." Recent research stated that one out of four American Protestants give away no money at all—not even a token $5 a week." [143] And we should keep in mind that even the poorest of the poor Americans are much better off than about 99% of the rest of the world. Evangelicals tend to be the most generous, but they do not outperform their peers enough to wear a badge of honor. Thirty-six percent report that they give away less than 2% of their income. Only about 27% tithe.[144]

But what would happen if we all set a tithe as the minimum of our giving? In 2008, Oxford University Press published a book called *Passing the Plate*. [145] In it, researchers say committed American Christians—those who say their faith is very important to them and those who attend church at least twice a month—earn more than $2.5 trillion dollars every year. That's astounding. It means that on their own, these Christians could be admitted to the *Group of Seven*, the group of the world's seven largest economies. Smith and his coauthors estimate that if these Christians gave away 10 percent of their after-tax earnings,

---

141 Acts 17:6 (NKJV)
142 1 Corinthians 3:12-15
143 Ref: sociologists Christian Smith, Michael Emerson, and Patricia Snell in a new study on Christian giving.
144 The tithe (or one-tenth) is usually seen as the bench mark minimum for biblical giving
145 "Passing the Plate - Why American Christians Don't Give Away More Money" by Christian Smith, Michael O Emerson and Patricia Snell – Oxford University Press 2008

they would add another $46 billion to ministries around the world. However, it could be argued that this is an underestimated amount. If you calculate that 10 percent of Christians don't give because of their financial limitations, and that most of the rest give 10 percent, there is also a group of generous givers who donate more than their expected tithe. This leads researchers to believe that American Christians could realistically increase their giving by $85.5 billion each year. [146]

"Money isn't everything," I hear you cry. And it isn't. All I ask is that we continue our little game of comparing ourselves and our present condition with that of the Early Church, of whom it was said, "All the believers were together and had everything in common. Selling their possessions and goods, they gave to anyone as he had need." [147] Consequently, "There were no needy persons among them. For from time to time those who owned lands or houses sold them, brought the money from the sales and put it at the apostles' feet, and it was distributed to anyone as he had need." [148]

We are shaped by our values and priorities. Just as the kingdom of God is a kingdom of priorities which must be placed 'first' above all other things, [149] so our lives take on the shape of our chosen values. My wife Jean and I have always ordered our lives that way. The first check made out, before bills are paid and food is bought, is the check representing our tithe, plus some additional offerings to support several aspects of ministry. Our approach to tithing is to be suitably grateful that we are asked to be stewards of the other 90%. Our greatest expenditure of energy and interest is for the kingdom of God. What a waste to be shaped otherwise. What a risk!

---

146   From, "Scrooge Lives" – Christianity Today – April 2, 2012
147   Acts 2:44-47
148   Acts 4:33-35
149   Matthew 6:33

Life Group Discussion
Chapter 12: What Shape, the Church?

The 'shape' of the Church speaks of its make-up and its ability to respond to everything and anything God calls it to be and do.

Questions for Discussion

Let's make a list of the Church's priorities – it's most significant values – its reason and purpose on earth. Now, let's ask the question of this chapter:

1. *"If the church was a fresh idea, birthed out of the first half of the 21st Century, what shape would it take"* to best fulfill that purpose?

Bill wrote, *"I believe the shape of the Church should be as flexible and multi-faceted as that of the New Testament."*

2. In what ways do you think the N.T. Church was more flexible than we might be? What changes can we make to "flex up?"

It's inevitable that our Life Groups are like another "meeting". Bill said, *"Although their purpose is to be more intimate than a public gathering, cell groups (we call them Life Groups) in the Church have an amazing way of becoming mini-meetings."*

3. What do you think he meant by that? What's wrong with another meeting? In what ways can we ensure that our small groups in the Church go deeper than public meetings ever can?

The scriptures tell us, *"There were no needy persons among them. For from time to time those who owned lands or houses sold them, brought the money from the sales and put it at the apostles' feet, and it was distributed to anyone as he had need."*

4. In what ways can your congregation grow in its ability to care for members with this level of love and commitment?

The statements in this chapter about the financial potential of the Church in the Western World are both inspiring and shocking!

5. Are you satisfied with the giving patters of your congregation? Do you see the tithe as the basic minimum of Christian giving? Pray for each other before you leave, asking God to pour His blessing not only on each member of your congregation, but also on their ability to pour blessing on others through godly giving.

13

Just Where Is the Mission Field?

When I was a child I could map out a pretty accurate world atlas, never dreaming I would ever get to travel to so many of the places I outlined on my maps. If the Pacific looked a bit empty in my drawings I would invent new islands, name them, chart the rivers and locate the cities. Looking back I can see that God was putting a passion for the nations into my young heart.

When I was seventeen – a year before entering into full-time ministry – I asked my parents if we could save up enough to buy me a vacation somewhere outside of England. For the British equivalent of about $50 I travelled to San Sebastian in the northwest corner of Spain. My Scottish parents had never left England during their long years of ministry so I contented myself with the thought that at least I had 'seen the world' before settling in to a static ministry-life in the UK. Little did I know what God had planned. Within weeks of entering Bible College I started traveling, and in these fifty years of ministry I have visited more than thirty nations. What a privilege, to see the Body of Christ in so many different places - such diversity and yet such faithful consistency.

The Church – there is nothing like it in all the earth. No government or business can come close. I work for the greatest organization in history. One day it will be the only surviving organization on the planet. Nothing that takes place in the White House or at number 10 Downing Street is as significant as that which was, is and will be enacted by God's Spirit, through the Church. [150] But it is my passionate love for the Church that provokes an equally profound frustration at so much of what we are, what we do, and what we *don't* do, and this privilege of ministering to the Church elsewhere in the world does not help my frustration. If you think it's a challenge to compare our Western Church with that of the New Testament era, it is just as challenging to hold ourselves up for comparison with the Church elsewhere, in our own generation.

It is sobering to hear how believers in nations where the Church is under constant threat are praying for us in the Western World. They know full well we have gone soft. We have begun to take for granted that which is a privilege of grace. In North America and Europe we have lived for so long under the impression that Christendom still exists. We tell ourselves that we are a Christian nation, founded on Christian principles, but this has lulled us into complacent inaction. Like the children of the Tsar in the days before the revolution we have forgotten that privilege comes with weighty responsibility. We think we have no need to fight for our identity or existence; no need for a Christian Jihad. [151] Our complacency has bred an aura of entitlement, allowing us to imagine that the adage, "insanity is doing the same thing over and over again and expecting different results," somehow doesn't apply to us. Is there any greater crime than taking God's grace for granted? I believe the anthem of the contemporary Western Church should be, "Don't it always seem to go that you don't know what you've got 'til it's gone." I shudder to think of what a loving God might have to do to waken His Church from its complacency!

---

150 Ephesians 3:10

151 The root of the word "jihad" is "juhd" which means "effort." Another related word is "ijtihad" which means "working hard or diligently."   Reference: *www.quranicstudies.com*

When I take teams out to other countries where there is abject poverty and little hope of social improvement, I often say, "If we didn't have money, what would we be bringing them?" There is an assumption that because we have money, which the Churches in so many countries have little or none of, we think this entitles us to be the benevolent bosses, the provisioning saviors, their superiors. But money means very little in God's kingdom and on earth it is no more than a tool.

Turn up to most African nations with a fist full of dollars and you will be treated like ecclesiastical royalty. But be careful! Having money to hand around doesn't make you an apostle. They will immediately call you 'Dad', and although it may be said as a genuine expression of gratitude and affection, in Africa that also means 'my provider'. So, before you assume some place of authority, you'd better have something other than cash in your bank. My advice would be to enter the so-called 'mission field' in abject humility, because you'll probably learn more than you can teach and receive much more than you can ever give away.

And just where is this 'mission field'? We do a serious disservice to our own judgment by talking of the Church in other countries as being the mission field when in reality we are leaving the mission field of post-Christian America or England to travel to places where the Church is more committed, more mature, more dedicated, more active and more... well, you get the point.

How did this happen? How did the traditionally Christian nations of the Western World arrive at a point where those darkened pagan points of missionary endeavor have taken their place as leaders of contemporary Christendom? It happened gradually, and like the frog boiling slowly in the pan of water, we haven't noticed the change in temperature.

The main cause of our undoing is in the very essence of our gospel. It is the Christian message that brings individual value, dignity and personhood to every human being. But this same message, which speaks of the freedom of the will and the creativity of personal responsibility also allows for individualism, and that leads to independence and pluralism in thought, word and deed. A pluralistic society allows us to think for ourselves. We are not ready to be coerced or cajoled into a box prescribed by either tradition or doctrine. It yells, "Question authority, question tradition, question everything!" It is this same personal liberty that drives us to invent, create and initiate, but it also allows us to rebel and ignore valuable lessons already learned by our predecessors.

I spend wonderful seasons in the Church in West Africa. There the culture is profoundly different from that of the West.

"If I put something on the table," said my friend Philipson Nagbe, a father in the faith to hundreds of churches throughout Liberia, "and I tell my guys,[152] 'Don't touch this,' they will not touch it."

"That's great," I replied. "But if I put something on the table and said that to my guys, they would immediately pick it up to inspect it, saying, 'Why, what's wrong with it?'" We both laughed. That inquisitive initiative is the American way, but it's also an opportunity for our darker angels.

When someone enters one of our meetings in Monrovia, the capital city of Liberia, (sadly renamed by 19th century Americans from its original glorious name, Cristapolis,)[153] they will be directed to a seat with the purposeful wave of an usher's hand. In the West I doubt that would go down too well. "We'll sit where we want, thank you!" Our cultures are markedly different. Would we want to trade our ingenuity and inventiveness for the African way? But we must ask, is the African way merely mindless obedience or is it a sign of a deep sense of respect for

---

152   Philipson's loving way of referring to a dozen or so leaders of churches throughout the country with whom he works
153   Cristapolis = City of Christ

authority? One thing is clear; it can be used to God's glory or abused as the opiate of the people. Independence, on the other hand, may be the mother of initiative and creativity, but it can also allow an inordinate opportunity for the enemy.

The Church outside the Western World has qualifications other than the obvious cultural differences with our lifestyle. Abject poverty and persistent persecution are often present; things which few of us have experienced. Ours battles pale beside theirs. "We are afraid of the jeer," wrote C. S. Lewis. In fact that fear has silenced us to the point of paralysis. The idea of being laughed at is enough to persuade most Western Christians to keep their beliefs to themselves – which is exactly what the world (and the devil) would prefer. Not for us the constant threat of persecution. Not yet, at least.

All this begs another question, in which environment does the Church most flourish; in the heat of serious life-threatening persecution, or in the tepid waters of cynical criticism or disinterested tolerance? We all know the answer, but we'd rather not tempt God to display it in our neighborhood! The persecuted Church, the impoverished Church, the underground and unaccepted Church throughout the world is exploding and vigorous, while the tolerated Church, the institutional Church, the Church which for too long has assumed its place in Western culture, is weak by comparison. Some of the great mega bastions of faith in America, which can easily spend many times more than Monrovia's annual city budget on a small addition to their worship center, too often manage only a pale reflection of the level of discipleship found in the dirt and dust of Liberia's tin-shack Churches. So, who's in charge here; the man with the money or the man with the disciples?

Paul knew of this level of discipleship in the Churches of his day. He described the Church in Macedonia in these terms, "Out of the most severe trial, their overflowing joy and their extreme poverty welled up in rich generosity. For I testify that they gave as much as they were able, and even beyond their ability. Entirely on their own, they urgently pleaded with us for the privilege of sharing in this service to the saints." [154] Sounds good, doesn't it. But we need to appreciate the extreme words he is using to describe their plight. The original language for 'extreme poverty' was *bathos ptocheia,* which means a profound state of indigence, even beggary! [155] And yet he witnessed such character in the midst of their plight, even to the point of overflowing joy and generosity beyond reason!

Discipleship is another word for disciplined commitment and allegiance, and these qualities are expressions of faithfulness, all of which are found within the Western Church, but how difficult it is to maintain these qualities in a culture which prides itself on individualism, independence and self-sufficiency. The ultimate outcome of a free pluralistic society goes beyond mere tolerance of the beliefs of others; it demands that everyone is his own teacher and, ultimately, that there can be no absolute of truth. "What is true for you isn't necessarily true for me. I'll decide what *my* truth is." This philosophy of convenience may be opposed to the foundations of the Church, but it is commonly found within her. Members who "vote with their feet" and keep the back door of their Church well oiled are playing it by the world's standards. Paul would have said they are not "rightly discerning the Body of Christ". In modern terms they are 'disrespecting the Body!'

It is interesting and shocking to see the climate within the Church in the nations where it is opposed. Those cultures which we call the 'mission field' are flourishing at a rate of which we can only dream. At the beginning of the 20th Century it was estimated that a mere 10% of Christians lived in the south and east of the planet. By the dawn of the 21st Century that number had risen to 70%. In "Church History in Plain Language," [156] Bruce Shelley claims that more Anglicans (or

---

154 2 Corinthians 8:2-4

155 Strong's Number NT:4432; New Exhaustive Strong's Numbers and Concordance with Expanded Greek-Hebrew Dictionary. Copyright © 1994, 2003 Biblesoft, Inc. and International Bible Translators, Inc.

156 "Church History in Plain Language" by Bruce L. Shelley – Published by Thomas Nelson

Episcopalians) meet in Nigeria each Sunday than in all of Britain, Europe and the United States combined. There are more members of the Assemblies of God in Latin America than in the U.S., and more Baptists in the Congo than in Britain.

I visited a pastor high in the Andes. Mount Chimborazo loomed over us on the near horizon, and he told me of the days when he would be attacked by Roman Catholics, sometimes stoned on his way to conduct a service for what was then a small and struggling congregation. A tiny Roman Catholic Church stood opposite us, across the traditional town square of all Latin communities.

"Now the priest comes only twice a year to minister Mass to a few older people," my friend said. "But we have 450 families attending our ministry."

The explosion of the Evangelical and Pentecostal church in Central and South America is phenomenal. It is unusual for my pastor friends in the Verbo churches of Ecuador to have fewer than 1,000 members in their congregations. One pastor showed us the building he was renovating for a new Church plant in the same city where they already had a congregation.

"We have to take a place this large," he said. "It must be able to seat 1,000." I heard some time later that it was filled within a few months of the launch.

The Verbo Church in Cuenca, which ministers to its community through a contemporary radio station, a children's home and a full service hospital, sees "about 35 people" joining them – each week! One mid-week evening I and my fellow team members of Alliance International Ministries [157] were presenting a leaders' training session in Verbo Cuenca. As the session progressed several people came in off the street to join the 200 or so leaders of that one local Church. This is

---

157   AIM – Online: "aimteam.org"

not unusual, I thought. Maybe they just got in late from work or they were delayed getting buses to the meeting. The meeting concluded with us laying hands on the leaders and some of those who had walked in late stepped forward for prayer. It was only as they asked for prayer that we discovered they were not leaders of the church at all; not even members. They had just "walked in off the street." They so enjoyed what they heard – and remember it was a leaders' training session – that they wanted to give their lives to Christ and join in!

The level of discipleship in our Liberian Churches would be a shock to the system of Western Christians. I sat in a leaders' meeting in Monrovia when Pastor Philipson Nagbe declared his concern over one new convert.

"I am worried about him. He has been saved for six months and he has not started a Cell Group."

"Wow, you expect him to do that?" I said, from my perspective of Western Church life.

"If a new convert does not start a cell group in his house," replied Philipson, "it means his testimony is not strong in his neighborhood." And to think, I was there to teach *them*!

In his book, "The Next Christendom: The Coming of Global Christianity," Philip Jenkins says, "Christianity as a whole is both growing and mutating in ways that observers in the West tend not to see .... (N)ews reports today are filled with material about the influence of a resurgent and sometimes angry Islam. But in its variety and vitality, in its global reach, in its association with the world's fastest-growing societies, in its shifting centers of gravity ... it is Christianity that will leave the deepest mark on the 21st century." He continues, "If we look beyond the liberal West, we see ... another Christian revolution," Jenkins reports. "Worldwide, Christianity is actually moving toward supernaturalism (and) the ancient worldview expressed in the New Testament: a vision of Jesus as the embodiment of divine power, who overcomes the evil forces that inflict calamity and sickness upon the human race. In the global South ... huge and growing Christian populations (now comprise) a form of Christianity as distinct as Protestantism or Orthodoxy, and one that is likely to become dominant in the faith." [158]

Perhaps the most amazing expression of the contemporary Church is the giant limb of the Body of Christ in Communist China, where more people attend Church on any given Sunday than in all of Europe. A typical expression of the vitality of this massive body of people is their expectation that they will be called on to evangelize not only the West but also the Muslim world. They speak of a "Back to Jerusalem" movement which reflects their understanding that Christ's command to take the gospel to the uttermost parts of the earth was fulfilled when the good news arrived in China. That, however, did not mean the job was done, so they are determined to 'advance' the gospel all the way back to Jerusalem. The prospect of a million Chinese missionaries advancing through Asia, the Middle East, Europe, and onto the shores on The New World is heart-warming indeed!

If we were to ask, "Will the real Church please stand up," would there be a great thundering of feet from parts of the world we still naively call 'the mission field' and a meek shuffling from Europe and North America?

Look again at what Jenkins said: "Worldwide, Christianity is actually moving toward supernaturalism (and) the ancient worldview expressed in the New Testament: a vision of Jesus as the embodiment of divine power, who overcomes the evil forces that inflict calamity and sickness upon the human race."

---

158   "The Coming of Global Christianity" by Philip Jenks – Oxford University Press, 2002.

If we were to compare the Church of the New Testament and that of the old missionary territories, we would find one similarity. In the Early Church and the regions where there is present growth, we find an acceptance of what Jenkins called *Supernaturalism;* the experience of the miraculous as an ongoing lifestyle. However, if the supernatural invades the Western Church it's called a Revival or an Outpouring and usually lasts but a few months, until we become wearied by its over-exposure on TV, Internet and Christian magazines, and so we discard it until the next trend hits the market.

I regularly visit people who have a very simple approach to life – their choices consist of basic, unsophisticated questions: "Do we buy paint for our walls, or do we eat? Do we buy books for our children, or food?" Life gets remarkably simple in such situations. In the same way they must ask, "When I am sick, will God heal me?" There are no alternatives. Not for them the expectation of healing from a doctor, a hospital, or even an Aspirin. It's God, or nothing. Elsewhere in our far reaching parish, back in the First World, the healing power of God is often the last resort. All else has failed, the doctors are perplexed, we're getting desperate here – we'd better throw ourselves on God.

Perhaps those martyrs were no better than we might have been, in simi-lar circumstances, and a few years in the U.S. can often turn the simple faith of an African believer into an acculturated shadow of his former self. What those martyrs had and what our westernized African might lose is desperation, a quality we need only *in extremis*. We all know we should seek the kingdom of God first, before any other resource, ahead of any other plan, but the fact is we have trained ourselves to be self reliant. It's as if we believe we'd be bothering God if we came with every little complaint or difficulty. We recall that God has said, "I am the Lord, the God of all mankind. Is anything too hard for me?" [159] So we only approach Him with the really hard stuff – when all else has failed. We 'believe for healing' when it's cancer. We take a pill when it's the

---

159 Jeremiah 32:27

flu. God is our God of our last resort. It is interesting to note that faith is described as a shield, [160] something to be used before the attack. We tend to exercise it after the fact, when all else has failed, but it's hard to get arrows out of your body…with a shield!

It has been said that desperate people seek God and lay hold of Him. God has said, "You will seek me and find me when you seek me with all your heart." [161] Jesus said, "Love the Lord your God with all your heart and with all your soul and with all your mind." [162] That sounds like desperation to me. Desperate people see revival. Desperate people spend time in anxious prayer. But it's hard to be desperate when there's little in life that causes desperation. When all is relatively tranquil, we are employed, the bills are being paid, the marriage is intact, the kids are not rebelling, Church life is satisfying and all our ducks are in a row and even Hell is under review, we would have to show remarkable maturity to get desperate… for the lost, for revival, for God.

When the call goes out for an all-night of prayer we may justify our slight pangs of guilt with the logic of, "Yeah, but some of us have to work in the morning," with a sideways nod to the pastor whose work it is to attend this sort of event. If, however, a gang of extremist idiots knocks down a couple of iconic towers in New York City, we'll get desperate enough to join our Church family in prayer. There might even be a groundswell of unity across the Body in the region as believers turn toward each other for comfort and to give expression to that mystical but oh-so-powerful desire for *sumphoneo*. For a season we might even catch a glimpse of what real Church is all about. But don't worry, it'll pass. Desperation is hard to maintain in a culture of a thousand comforts.

---

160 Ephesians 6:16
161 Jeremiah 29:13
162 Matthew 22:37

Life Group Discussion
Chapter 13: Just Where Is the Mission Field?

This chapter speaks of the wonderful gift God has given us; our freedom to choose, initiate and create. But that same freedom can breed a society that refuses to conform to anything, even the essentials of God's laws for life and relationship with Him and with each other. Bill says, "How difficult it is to maintain the qualities of discipleship, commitment and agreement in a culture which prides itself on individualism, independence and self-sufficiency."

Questions for discussion

1. How can we be convinced to walk as true disciples, submitting ourselves to God, to the authority of the Church and to one another, while still maintaining that creative individualism so beloved by the Western World? What character qualities are required to do this in a way that is pleasing to God?

Whereas Bill is a firm believer – and active participant – in trips to help and encourage socially, educationally and financially deprived parts of the Body of Christ, this chapter suggests that we've got it skewed when we speak of the 'mission field', *"when in reality we are leaving the mission field of post-Christian America or England to travel to places where the Church is more committed, more mature, more dedicated, more active and more… well, you get the point."*

2. Do you agree with this assessment? What evidence does Bill give that this is the case? How does this affect our understanding of the place of the Church in our society? Could we missionaries, every day?

3. Bill asked the question, *"in which environment does the Church most flourish; in the heat of serious life-threatening persecution, or*

in the tepid waters of cynical criticism or disinterested tolerance?"
What is your answer?

4. Is it possible for the Western Church to regain its passion without having to suffer persecution, opposition, deprivation and the other things which so often attend the most virile expressions of modern and historical Christianity?

5. Why is it that we tend to be passionate (hot) in times of pressure and complacent (lukewarm) in times of plenty? What can we do to change this? What can keep our passion alive?

Let's finish our time together by reading Jeremiah 29:11-14 and Matthew 22:35-40. After we read these verses we should pray for one another, that the embers of passion for God and for souls might be fanned into flame in each of our hearts and in the Body of Christ in the Western World.

14

The Long and Winding Road

I've spent many years looking over my shoulder, not in fear, but in the hope that a group of young people might one day say, "Sorry, Bill, but we need to go higher, deeper, father and faster than you can take us." It hasn't happened yet, but I live in hope that the Church will once more be filled with shameless young idealists who truly believe God meant what He said when He promised to show his wisdom in all its rich variety "through the Church" to all the rulers and authorities in the heavenly realms. [163]

Our God is still the same as in the days of the New Testament Church and we are much the same as those first followers of The Way. We are still saved by grace and not by works of our own doing. We are still rebellious fools and He still insists He will turn us into "His body, the fullness of him who fills everything in every way." [164] It's still the case that "few of you were wise in the world's eyes, or powerful, or wealthy when God called you. Instead, God deliberately chose things the world considers foolish in order to shame those who think they are wise. And he chose those who are powerless to shame those who are powerful. God chose things despised by the world; things counted as nothing

---

163 Ephesians 3:10
164 Ephesians 1:23

at all, and used them to bring to nothing what the world considers important, so that no one can ever boast in the presence of God." [165] It's still true that God loves to choose and mightily use what men think nothing at all. The scum of the earth!

Jesus spent a lot of time with such "scum". Celsus wrote in his work, 'True Discourse,' [166] "Their aim is to convince only worthless and contemptible people, idiots, slaves, poor women, and children.... These are the only ones they manage to turn into believers." Not too complimentary and not at all true, but imagine your congregation being described that way in the local press!

There is still passion in the Church of the Western World. It becomes especially evident when believers are sprung out into 'the mission field,' but too often the same people are paralyzed, submissive and dormant, back home. Perhaps Western Christians have believed the lie of Satan that the world has passed them by and that they now live in a "Post Christian" era. But this world has as much chance of being 'Post Christian' as it does of existing 'Post Christ'. He is the "Alpha *and* the Omega, the beginning and the end." [167] There's nothing after Him. When He ends it, that's it! He'll be there, and so will we, and no-one else.

We've taken a long and winding road in these chapters, from the close of the Old Testament, through the exciting birth of the Church, on through the often grimy but always glorious pages of Church History and into the present age of incredible Church growth in the most unexpected places. So, what now? Where does the Church in this tired Western World go from here? Let me to conclude with my thoughts – my hopes.

I started out as a young 1960s revolutionary for the cause of Christ.

---

165 1 Corinthians 1:26-29 (New Living Translation)
166 'True Reason' as a polemic against the Christians in approximately 178 A.D.
167 Revelation 1:8; 21:6; 22:13

Back then we did things that didn't only rock the boat; some wished we would jump ship. The Jesus Revolution of the 1970s started a decade after I had come into ministry. I was baptized in the Spirit around the same age that Jesus started His ministry. No... I said 'around the same *age*' not 'around the same *time*'! The Jesus Revolution saw thousands of young people sold out to Christ. We were ready to go anywhere and do anything for Him. Who could refuse the greatest privilege on the planet – which also turned out to be the most fun? We lived together, sometimes several families to a small English house. We traveled the Middle East, living wherever we could find a spot to pitch our tents. We once parked forty missionaries in the center of a traffic island in Crete, our young children with us. Those same kids came to evening meetings in their 'pudgies' (pajamas) and fell asleep watching the Holy Spirit move in power. Our kids also learned to walk silently and secretly into apartment buildings for clandestine meetings with believers behind the Iron Curtain. Their earliest schooling was conducted sitting under palm trees, often with the pyramids in the background or with the Wailing Wall of Solomon's Temple as a backdrop. They could have been back safely in an English school room, but they were fortunate enough to have parents who thought it best to go wherever Jesus told them.

Out of the Jesus Revolution came the Charismatic Renewal and the Church world-wide was and is transformed. Thousands of young people stepped out and planted Churches, travelled the globe, opened ministries. For most it was 'learn as you go – trust the Holy Spirit'. However, this has left the Western Church with one of its greatest challenges. Thousands grew up and learned their trade in ministries they had planted themselves, whether local Churches or world-wide explosions such as Youth With A Mission. But that generation - those who were once reckless 'kids' - are now grandparents, looking for 'sons and daughters of the house' to take on the family business. It is one thing to start fresh, inexperienced, raw, and grow up in the ministry; it's quite another thing to fill Dad's (or Granddad's) shoes. And maybe Dad's shoes simply don't fit anymore. They were, after all, cobbled in another era – another world.

So, what happens now? Where do we go from here? What shape, the Church of the 21st Century? What qualities may we look for to impact this world of ours? Is there another Jesus Revolution around the next corner? There'd better be, or we will die! So, here's what I'm asking God for… my strategies for the Church of the 21st Century.

1. Sold-Out Madness

A generation of Christians needs to be raised up with that same sold-out madness for the kingdom of God that causes the effects of the 60s and 70s still to be felt today.

We need the kind of strategic and sacrificial passion we often see in other cultures whose people may not have our expectations of comfort and entitlement. Take, for instance, the group of young men from India who came to America. They lived together in one home – all working – all paying their wages into a common pool, just like the New Testament Church. Each year, one of them was launched out into business, funded from the pool. He continued to contribute to the group purse even as his business grew through its early stages. The others continued in their jobs. Each year, another was launched out. It took about a decade until every one of them owned their own business; hotels, convenience stores, gas stations. Then, they sent for their families! You may have wondered why all those hotels and convenience stores are owned by Asians. Now you have some idea. It's called hard work and sacrifice. That leads us to strategy number two.

2. Sacrificial Living

This coming generation must be ready to commit itself to strategic lifestyles that are flexible enough to see the kingdom come. Not one penny of debt was incurred by those Indian friends. Nor was one day spent in College, or one dime spent *on* College!

We suffer from a plague in the United States – it's an epidemic of entitlement. Many kids are led to believe that Mom and Dad owe them a place in college - fully funded - and a car to get them to school in which they can bring their laundry home at weekends. Parents are to blame, of course. They wouldn't be admired by their peers if they failed in this duty. Entitlement demands that the very best comes my way with the minimum or work on my part. It's disgusting. It breeds ego-centered 26-year-old adolescents who lack vision, direction and purpose – and a job! The kingdom of God is all about service and sacrifice, and it's much more fun than all that "me" stuff!

As the founder of The King's School,[168] a life-long student, and a teacher of many years, I am a strong believer in preparing tomorrow's leaders today through excellence in education, but not an education which leaves young people passion-less and vision-deprived. Like generations past, few of our young people know what they're going to be when they grow up, but one thing they *will* be is 'in debt'. Debt is the greatest hindrance in our Western World to the ability to say "Here am I, my Lord, send me." [169]

Young people today are just as ready to hear from God and obey Him as in any previous generation. The question is not *will* they, it is *can* they? We stepped out without a penny, but also without a penny of debt. Not one step of our ministry could have been taken had we been obligated to a college loan, or a car loan, or a credit card debt. We have a simple approach to finance. We believe in G.O.O.D. finance; Get Out Of Debt! Not only because it's expensive, but also because it's bondage.

---

168   Visit www.kingsschool.info
169   Isaiah 6:8

Several of my colleagues have recently been involved with calling young people out into ministry, only to be met with the minimum demands required to cover the lifestyle already established in the young people's lives. Imagine trying to start out in ministry with a huge college loan. Sorry kids, one of these days Jesus is going to call you out of the boat to walk on the water, and becoming financially free enough to obey Him doesn't mean putting all your stuff into foreclosure!

Imagine a congregation of believers who form their Church life on the priorities of God's kingdom on earth, each member arranging all their social and familial obligations so that they are free to go anywhere for Jesus, at the drop of a hat.

3.   A Heart of Compassion

Imagine that same congregation giving themselves to the joy of winning one person to Christ each year; just one. When it comes to our expectations, surely 'one' must be the minimum. It's almost embarrassing to suggest that we need the passion, compassion and vision enough to win 'one'.

Mention 'compassion' to any Salvationist of a certain age and he will think of one great song. In the summer of 1965 I stood on the stage of the Royal Albert Hall in London. The Joystrings had just finished participating in a massive rally of Salvationists. The crowd of many thousands was slowly milling out of the arena leaving one elderly gentleman standing at the front, looking up at us. This man was a retired General of The Salvation Army, a lovely man, a great preacher, a powerful poet, and the composer of that great song. He wrote:

> *The Savior of men came to seek and to save*
> *The souls who were lost to the good;*
> *His Spirit was moved for the world which he loved*
> *With the boundless compassion of God.*

And still there are fields where the laborers are few,
And still there are souls without bread,
And still eyes that weep where the darkness is deep,
And still straying sheep to be led.
O is not the Christ 'midst the crowd of today
Whose questioning cries do not cease?
And will he not show to the hearts that would know
The things that belong to their peace?
But how shall they hear if the preacher forbear
Or lack in compassionate zeal?
Or how shall hearts move with the Master's own love,
Without his anointing and seal?
Except I am moved with compassion, how dwelleth thy Spirit in me?
In word and in deed burning love is my need;
I now know I can find it in thee. [170]

4. Godly Dissatisfaction

I have already spoken of the emptiness I felt at the end of an eleven year period of ministry, even though my 'career' had been launched to a magnificent degree. After those years of travel, television, concert halls, adulation and applause, I felt like "an empty can of words". [171] One day I sat alone in my car at the crossroads at the center of Newark in the very middle of England. I stared out the front windshield and said, "There has to be more than this." I'm not sure if I said it to myself or out loud. Either way, God heard.

One of my favorite songs begins, *"There must be more than this, O breath of God, come breathe within."* [172]

Whereas I cried it out in the 1970s with a touch of desperation, I say it

---

170 Except I am Moved With Compassion - by   General Albert Osborne. Used by permission, Salvationist Publishing & Supplies
171 More of this testimony in   "Marked for Life" and "Choices" by Bill Davidson
172 Consuming Fire - by Tim Hughes. Used by permission, Thankyou Music

still, today, but with a touch of expectation. There's always 'more'. God is infinite – beyond measure. He's not stuck for ideas just because the world has changed. He is adaptable and creative. His unchangeableness is set firmly in His nature and character, but He can adapt to every vicissitude of mankind. A ministry that stays the same, yesterday, today and forever is probably completely out of touch with the Spirit of God who created it – if indeed He did!

5.   Godly Continuity

In Hadley, New York, the campus of The King's School welcomes in students, year after year, from congregations around our region, and even some from as far as Colombia and Ecuador. They think little of King's Road. It's the street that leads to their sports fields. Recently built homes stand on either side. It's just your average rural development in Upstate New York. But Jean and I think of it differently. We remember the day when we took out some orange surveyor's tape and tied it to a tree. One of us stood by that first tree while the other walked forward about 30 yards more, into dense forest; "Left a bit – a little to your right…yes, there!" And we tagged another tree, and so on until we had mapped the outline of what would one day be the road. A few months later a crowd of us walked that same line with chainsaws and logged out the road. Others followed to 'limb' the branches off the trunks and yet more came behind to stack fires to burn the brush. In three Saturdays the mile-long road took shape. The road – and the ministries that surrounded it – could not be born without vision first being in place.

None of us – however revolutionary or radical we might think ourselves to be – ever got anywhere without the faithfulness of others; even those with whom we became dissatisfied for their 'lack of vision' and their adherence to the status quo. In God's eyes, their faithfulness might outshine our zeal. That's why I never depreciate my days in The Salvation Army. We have been told we were 'thirty years ahead of our time' and the things in which we walked, which seemed so out-of-step with the Army in which we had grown up, are now enjoyed by thousands within the Movement. That matters little. We may have been square pegs in round holes, but we respect the holes!

Is it a worn out cliché to suggest that those who do not learn from history are condemned to repeat it? It's still true. We need more people like Elisha, who spent years serving an apostolic and prophetic ministry, then – as the older generation was obviously getting ready to leave – asked God for a double portion of the old guy's anointing. That double portion was required because Elisha knew he needed all the past could teach him, but he also knew he would face a whole new generation of enemies. [173]

In this way, the power of one generation's anointing becomes the launch pad for another's. But we don't always achieve such godly continuity. We allow ourselves to run down to the point of being dormant. Then we cry out for what we call 'Revivals'. They are wonderful things. I've enjoyed my share. But Revivals suggest the reawakening of something which is dead – or, at least, somewhat sleepy!

We also have these things called "Outpourings," and, yes, I have trooped up to Toronto with the rest of them and thoroughly enjoyed myself. I honor the integrity I found amongst the leaders of that 'well of refreshment!' We even exported some powerful times as we crossed back over the border between Ontario and New York. But I have to wonder whether God is tiring of our treatment of such seasons of refreshing, especially when, in some places, the blessing is turned into little more than a fleshly, self-centered palace of enjoyment. Sometimes God was in the place. At other times people flocked, by the thousands, bought books, by the millions, stood in adoration like the adoring Minions led by Despicable Me, as some of the most blatantly outrageous and ungodly happenings took place before their gullible eyes.

---

173   2 Kings 2:9-15

In all of our revolutions and revivals we have sometimes climbed to dizzy heights, only to tire of spiritual altitude sickness and settle on some summit, never realizing that we have been revived because there's a job to do somewhere down in the next valley. God once said to His people as they were comfortably camped, forgetful of the very reason for their newly won freedom, "You have stayed long enough at this mountain. Break camp and advance into the hill country of the Amorites… Go in and take possession of the land that the Lord swore he would give to your fathers — to Abraham, Isaac and Jacob — and to their descendants after them." [174]

In other words, "I know you'd like to stay here, in camp, but there's a war on."

Peter suffered from that same syndrome at the time of Christ's transfiguration when he said, "Rabbi, it is good for us to be here. Let us put up three shelters — one for you, one for Moses and one for Elijah." Then a cloud appeared and enveloped them, and a voice came from the cloud: "This is my Son, whom I love. Listen to him!" [175] In other words, "Nice try, Peter, it would be cozy to stay up in the clouds of this revival, but there's a demonized boy in the next valley. Stay here, and he's on his way to Hell. Jesus is about to go and deliver him. Stop talking and listen to Him."

Can we believe for the kind of Godly continuity for this generation which will see constant, steady and deliberate growth, rather than the hills and valleys of revival, stagnation and the need for yet another revival? Could we attain to a place of maturity, learning from the past, honoring those who have apostolically paved the way before us, while at the same time, seizing the day and serving the purposes of God for our generation? Could we allow the Holy Spirit to do His work among us without keeping Him to ourselves, for our comfort and enjoyment?

---

174 Deuteronomy 1:6-8
175 Mark 9:5-7

Could we stop turning His presence into that of the main Performer at our meetings?

6.   More Lepers Required

Our response to the visitations of the Holy Spirit reminds me of those lepers in the time of Elisha. They stood outside a city which had been under siege for weeks. There they were, in their rags – the scum of the earth - stuck between the starving people in the city and the enemy in the valley. Eventually they decided that they might as well give up. "Let's go over to the camp of the enemy. If they spare us, we live; if they kill us, then we die." [176] I love that line! I've often spoken it to our congregation, adding "The very worst they can do to us is precipitate us – sooner than we expected – into the Presence of God!"

But when those lepers got there they found that the enemy had fled, leaving their tables fit for a feast. At first they gorged their hungry bellies on the good things arrayed before them. But then they realized their selfishness: They spoke words to each other which should be emblazoned on the walls of every church building: "We're not doing right. This is a day of good news and we are keeping it to ourselves." [177]

---

176   2 Kings 7:4
177   2 Kings 7:9

Life Group Discussion
Chapter 14: The Long and Winding Road

This chapter could pose many questions and you might want to spend time discussing some of its challenges, but in fact we are going to spend at least some of our time together praying specific prayers linked to the challenges the chapter provokes.

The Coming Jesus Revolution
Pray for the youth of the Body of Christ to be provoked by the Holy Spirit to see clearly the need for a Jesus-centered, sold-out revolution in the Church of this generation, filled with power and passion and blessed with wisdom and revelation.

Revivals and Outpourings
Pray for a new and deeper appreciation of God's purpose for refreshing and reviving His Church and for godly character, maturity, holiness and discernment to be the hallmark of the next awakening.

Godly Continuity
Pray for a generation of Elishas to be raised up; faithful servants, who will take the reins, grasp the baton and continue the race, showing honor for their apostolic roots but hearing God's clear strategies for this coming age.

More Lepers Required
Pray for the sold-out heart of those lepers when they said, "Now let us go into the camp of the enemy. If they spare us, we shall live. If they kill us, we shall but die."

Repentance
Ask for God's forgiveness for the times we have lived through the day of good news and kept it to ourselves. Ask for His grace and power to be poured out upon the Church of our generation to lovingly but definitely touch the lost.

15

Epilogue

It is a privilege beyond description to be a part of the Church, a limb of the Body of Christ. The Son of God really did go to Calvary just for me, but that doesn't mean it's only about me, or you; it's about the Church. It's about Jesus, the Head of the Church. It's about the purposes of God in our generation. It's about the only hope this world has. It's about an obedient Church doing what she is here on earth to do, and by this means, speeding His return [178] – nothing else, and nothing less.

I don't know how much longer I will be in His service, but I don't want to waste a day. So let me finish with a story that has stayed with me for years and if nothing else in this book has brought conviction, this one should get you! It happened when Jean and I took our children and a small team for the first time behind the Iron Curtain, into Communist Czechoslovakia. [179]

One afternoon we sat with about two dozen people who had come, without invitation, led by the Holy Spirit, to visit the house where we were staying, for one day only. It was a 'secret meeting', unannounced, but well attended! For some hours I spoke to these people who were

---

178 2 Peter 3:12
179 The full story of this trip can be found in the book, "Marked for Life" by Bill Davidson

Other Books by Bill Davidson

"MARKED FOR LIFE"
The Marks of a Man Who Has Met With God
Accompanying Small Group Manual
And Video Teaching Series

"CHOICES"
Stop Blaming God!
Accompanying Small Group Manual
And Video Teaching Series

Accompanying Small Group Video Teaching Series To
"IF PAUL WALKED IN TO YOUR CHURCH"

Available from BillDavidsonMedia
207 Sunnyside East
Queensbury, NY 12804

CPSIA information can be obtained at www.ICGtesting.com
Printed in the USA
BVOW080117250912

301219BV00001B/1/P